What people are saying about …

LOVE WELL

"I've always said that the best teachers are storytellers, and Jamie George is one of the best storytellers I know. I've been blessed by hearing him tell his stories in person for years. Now it's your turn!"

Dave Ramsey, *New York Times* bestselling author and nationally syndicated radio show host

"Jamie cuts through the religious stereotypes. His laid-back, transparent style of storytelling is extremely refreshing and encouraging for a guy like me, who was raised in the church and feels like he has seen it all. Jamie is a new friend that we all truly need to hear from."

Jeremy Cowart, photographer and founder of Help-Portrait

"Jamie has invited us into his life through this book. *Love Well* is a peek into a preferred future. You will be drawn in and challenged to live life in a way that glorifies God and brings you deep joy."

Darrin Patrick, lead pastor of The Journey, vice president of Acts 29, and author of *The Dude's Guide to Manhood*

"Jamie George is the most authentic communicator I have ever met. It is a privilege to have him not only as my pastor and spiritual teacher but also as my friend. Working under Jamie's leadership for the last seven years, I know that his story and his willingness to share from a place of brokenness will lead others to redemption and a deeper relationship with Jesus. It did for me. *Love Well* is a book about relationships and brokenness, of community and of the wholeness we are all stumbling toward. Once you immerse yourself in this breathtaking narrative, I believe you will be overcome with the beauty of a God who has designed us to love and be loved."

Leslie Jordan, All Sons & Daughters,
and worship leader at Journey Church

"When I heard Jamie was writing this book, my first thought was, at last! He's been one of my favorite storytellers for years, and as soon as you read *Love Well*, he'll be one of yours too."

Jon Acuff, *New York Times* bestselling
author of *Start* and *Stuff Christians Like*

"I need real. Don't you? When it comes to love and faith and all the parts of life bubbling below the surface, I can't waste time on something that doesn't cut me to the core. It's this desire for authenticity that first drew me to Jamie's storytelling. No frills, no pretense ... messy human characters that are REAL people. Jamie's book arrived at a time in my life when I'm learning the difference between loving others and loving myself. What's selfish? What's self-care? What's unconditional? Help! Let's be honest, when are any of us not absolutely dying to love and be loved well?"

Hayley Williams, of the band Paramore

"Truth is something we don't hear much anymore. Everything is hype, marketing, or just packaged lies to get us to believe in something. *Love Well* is filled with real truth that will challenge what you think about religion, forgiveness, and your own personal story."

Randy Brewer, executive producer
at Revolution Pictures

"In *Love Well*, George offers us a spiritual harvest of connection— with God, ourselves, and others—so we can wade through our stuck places and start moving again. The poignant story of his marriage will move you. His superb writing will inspire you. His insights will challenge you."

Mark Batterson, *New York Times* bestselling author of *The Circle Maker*

"*Love Well* is a hard book to put down. Jamie George's transparency lends a much-needed, fresh voice to issues of love, particularly within the urban context. This book is a timely, relevant, and effective tool that will undoubtedly liberate many to live and love richly."

Dimas Salaberrios, pastor of Infinity
Bible Church and president of Concerts
of Prayer of Greater New York

"Jamie George has been my pastor, mentor, and friend for many years. His willingness to be both open and honest, as well as his genuine love for people sets him apart. To *Love Well* should be our daily mission as followers of Jesus. God so beautifully paints a picture of what that looks like through Jamie's story."

Brandi Cyrus, model, host, and actress

"A consummate narrative weaver, Jamie has moved that gift into the pages of *Love Well*. Many readers will be unfamiliar with the resources he skillfully weaves with biblical and personal story, making this an unexpected but beautifully textured tapestry. There will be threads you want to pursue on their own and others that simply look gorgeous as they sit in these pages. I hope his first foray of loom-work will create better lovers—and lots of them. He deserves to be heard and read."

Dr. Ron Martoia, author and speaker for Velocity Culture

"Jamie George doesn't stand idly by and point you in the direction your life should go, but rather he vulnerably walks beside you and creatively, clearly, and concisely inspires you toward what it means to *Love Well*."

Joel Smallbone, of the band
for KING & COUNTRY

"As childhood friends that reconnected as adults, both in ministry, it has been a joy to see the way God has used Jamie to bring hope to others. His writing and his life reflect his passion to *Love Well!*"

Robert Stearns, executive director of Eagles Wings

"Masterful storyteller Jamie George takes a bold, vulnerable, and worthwhile approach in exposing the kinks and cracks of his marriage to offer insight in getting unstuck. This book doesn't give generic or cliché answers (thankfully). Through artful illustrations, George does provoke the reader to self-reflection. Sometimes the response will be painful, sometimes ugly, sometimes breathtakingly beautiful."

A. J. Gregory, *New York Times* bestselling coauthor of *Nowhere But Up, Messy Faith,* and *Silent Savior*

"*Love Well* offers you a map and tools to negotiate a journey into a foreign land most American Christians have never visited. This journey is dangerous, painful, and demands discipline. To enter its gates means you will have to leave behind hiding, arrogance, pride, self-righteousness, and legalism forever. For many of you it will ask you to do something you have avoided your entire life: be vulnerable and exposed to the world. For the few who have the courage to venture through the trail Jamie and his wife have blazed for you, you might just find that your story in Christ is more magnificent than you have ever experienced before."

Brad Stine, actor, comedian, and "God's Comic" for the *New Yorker*

"Jamie's honesty and vulnerability in *Love Well* continue to inspire me. Every time I pick it up, I find more. My life is being shaped by the powerful insight in this book."

David Leonard, All Sons & Daughters,
and worship leader at Journey Church

"Jamie George is a masterful storyteller with a penchant for real-life situational significance. I've never felt comfortable with church or its confines, but I am proud to call Jamie my pastor, friend, and fellow artist."

Kevin Max, artist and author, formally
with DC Talk & Audio Adrenaline

"Jamie George has a heart that beats for believers in Jesus to live an authentic faith. I am a regular listener to his podcast, have had the privilege to be a part of his services in Nashville, and believe him to be one of the men God is raising up in our generation to bring loving truth and clarity. He's also simply a cool guy. You'd want to hang out with him. The subject "love well" strikes a nerve inside me, because after a lifetime of being in the faith, I need to be reminded of just what it's all about in the first place."

Cliff Graham, bestselling author and
creator of the Lion of War franchise

"In *Love Well*, we are invited into a story that is raw, candid, and redemptive. Not only did I resonate with Jamie's struggle, but I found his reflections fresh, buoyant, and full of hope.

Jamie has been my friend for more than a decade. I've been telling him to write a book all that time. When you read it, you'll find out why."

Darren Whitehead, author (with Jon Tyson) of *Rumors of God* and lead pastor of Church of the City

"Jamie and I live on opposite sides of the earth, yet our stories have connected—connection, as he puts it, "watered in truth" that "blooms in the soil of vulnerability." Australians value truth (we call it being "fair dinkum"). We value compassion, too. We don't care what you know until we know that you care. *Love Well* has truth and grace, disclosure and sensitivity, prophetic edge and pastoral heart. If you're unsure of the spiritual realm, if you've been wounded by insensitive zeal or worn out on the religious treadmill, here are prompts to relationship with the One who weaves the broken and discordant elements of our stories together into vibrant harmony."

Graham Mabury, radio personality and pastor

"*Love Well* is one of those books that grips you from the beginning. Jamie and Angie show us that the abundant life is an honest life. *Love Well* will give any reader a road map to that honesty and as a result, a fuller, more satisfying life."

David Whitehead, author and founder of TheDailyBibleVerse.org

"I warn you, if you read this spiritual autobiography, the needle on the compass of your motivations will be spinning in directions you never dreamed of! Some of your favorite ways of relating will be flipped upside down. After reading *Love Well*, I believe you will find renewal in every one of the chapters. They build underneath you like pavers on a mountain road. You climb methodically and strongly with Jamie to find a breath of fresh grace."

Al Andrews, director of Porter's Call

LOVE WELL

LIVING LIFE UNREHEARSED AND UNSTUCK

JAMIE GEORGE

David C Cook®
transforming lives together

LOVE WELL
Published by David C Cook
4050 Lee Vance View
Colorado Springs, CO 80918 U.S.A.

David C Cook Distribution Canada
55 Woodslee Avenue, Paris, Ontario, Canada N3L 3E5

David C Cook U.K., Kingsway Communications
Eastbourne, East Sussex BN23 6NT, England

The graphic circle C logo is a registered trademark of David C Cook.

The website addresses recommended throughout this book are offered as a
resource to you. These websites are not intended in any way to be or imply an
endorsement on the part of David C Cook, nor do we vouch for their content.

Scripture quotations, unless otherwise noted, are taken from the Holy Bible, New
International Version®, NIV®. Copyright © 1973, 2011 by Biblica, Inc.™ Used by permission
of Zondervan. All rights reserved worldwide. www.zondervan.com. Scripture quotations
marked NLT are taken from the Holy Bible, New Living Translation, copyright © 1996,
2007 by Tyndale House Foundation. Used by permission of Tyndale House Publishers,
Inc., Carol Stream, Illinois 60188. All rights reserved; KJV are taken from the King James
Version of the Bible. (Public Domain.); ESV are taken from The Holy Bible, English
Standard Version® (ESV®), copyright © 2001 by Crossway, a publishing ministry of Good
News Publishers. Used by permission. All rights reserved; NASB are taken from the New
American Standard Bible®, Copyright © 1960, 1995 by The Lockman Foundation. Used
by permission. (www.Lockman.org.); MSG are taken from *THE MESSAGE*. Copyright
© by Eugene H. Peterson 1993, 2002. Used by permission of NavPress Publishing
Group; WNT are taken from the Weymouth New Testament Bible. (Public Domain.)
The author has added italics to Scripture quotations for emphasis.

LCCN 2014937604
ISBN 978-1-4347-0728-4
eISBN 978-0-7814-1163-9

© 2014 Jamie George
Published in association with the literary agency of The Fedd
Agency, Inc., Post Office Box 341973, Austin, Texas 78734.
The Team: Alex Field, A. J. Gregory, Amy Konyndyk, Nick Lee, Caitlyn Carlson, Karen Athen
Cover Design: Nick Lee
Cover Photo: Nick Lee

Printed in the United States of America
First Edition 2014

1 2 3 4 5 6 7 8 9 10

052814

To Angie:
Your teachable spirit, your courage, and
your willingness to share is incomparable.
Thank you for encouraging
me to tell our story.
We went looking for love, and it found us.

CONTENTS

ACKNOWLEDGMENTS

My children: Jordan, Tyler, Ashton, and Addison. My love and affection for you cannot be adequately expressed using words. As your father, it is a privilege to be included in your stories.

My father and mother, Rich and Sue. Of the many gifts you have given me I am thankful most for your love and the space to explore life. My love is full and overflowing for you both.

My sisters and brothers-in-law: Jodi and Darrick, Jineen and Shane, Joy and Mark. My gratitude for the consistent love exchange is never spoken enough.

My wife's family, the McIntyres, for their love and support.

Doyle Yarbrough, thank you for your rescue. You are a true guardian.

Paul Farmer, without your encouragement and creative gifts, the words that follow would still be wedged in the crevices of my heart.

Esther Fedorkevich, for believing in me and carrying this vision forward.

Amy Gregory Spence, for patient and insightful guidance. You are a Jedi.

Uli Reyes, for your unending generosity.

My friends and fellow travelers—you have encouraged me and inspired me:

Zach Gray, Marq James, Leslie Jordan, David Leonard, Terry and Susie Dunham, Scott and Taryn Hofert, Mark Stuart, Randy Brewer, Zach Prichard, Nick Barre, Karen Kingsbury, Dave Ramsey, Hunter Ingram, David Whitehead, Darren Tyler, Joel Smallbone, Gary and Trina Carter, Teresa Davis, Brent McCorkle, Hayley Williams, Don Pape, Alex Field, Rufus and Ruth Howe, Chris Motley, Robert Stearns, Jon Acuff, Cliff Graham, David Bruce and the University of the Nations in Kona, Hawaii, and the Abbey at Gethsemani in New Haven, Kentucky.

Eugene Peterson, Richard Rohr, Dallas Willard, Tim Keller, and Malcolm Gladwell, whose writings have mentored me in significant ways.

The Journey Church. You have courageously shared with me your stories and patiently loved me in mine.

FOREWORD

By Karen Kingsbury

Breakfast was at Cracker Barrel that early Sunday morning.

We straggled through the doors, tired from a cross-country move to Nashville, Tennessee, tired of living out of a hotel, the furniture four days behind us. Our family had one goal that day.

Find a church.

We met friends at the restaurant, and soon the topic turned to churches.

"Try Journey." They smiled. "Follow us. You'll love it."

Nashville is home to dozens of amazing churches, and we had a different one in mind that day. But after we finished up at Cracker Barrel, we followed our friends. We read about the church on my phone as my husband drove. Journey was a nondenominational church just south of Nashville in Franklin. The pastor was a man we hadn't heard of before.

Jamie George.

Something felt different about the place from the moment we walked in. An hour later, tears streamed down my face. My heart was raw, my soul wide open. Sitting beside me, my husband felt the same way. In a single sermon the gospel had come to life like never before. I wanted to rush back into the everyday world and love better, serve more.

I wanted to live my faith out loud.

I didn't feel stuck headed into Journey Church that Sunday morning. I've had great pastors in my life, godly men who taught me Scripture and challenged me to grow in my faith. But my faith found a new level of motion as I walked out the doors that day. I felt changed. Like God was ushering in a new level of living for Him. A new level of faith.

Faith as a verb.

Jamie's teaching came in stories. The fact is, some people were born to tell stories. The storytellers of our day. I like to say that when Jesus wanted to teach you something, He told you straight.

He overturned tables.

But when He wanted to touch your heart, He told a story.

Those who tell stories carry forward the beautiful love saga of Jesus. They paint color where previously there was only black and white. They help us see our part in the Great Story ... the one God invites us into. They put the dusty dirt of Jerusalem beneath our feet and let us experience the sounds of the temple courts. They help us hear the voice of God.

Jamie George is one of those storytellers.

We never looked at another church. Every Sunday my husband and I head to Journey with our five boys. Our daughter and son-in-law meet us there. Then our family settles in, hearts ready, and we listen. God speaks to us through Jamie.

Week after week after week.

Now it's your turn.

My prayer is that God will speak to you through Jamie too. This book is a piece of his heart—no filters. Just Jamie giving us a window to what God is doing in his life. Storytelling for us. Sharing his story.

So that we might better understand what God can do in ours.

Picking up this book just might change your life. The way step-ping through the doors of Journey Church our first Sunday in Nashville changed mine.

Best Cracker Barrel breakfast we ever had.

INTRODUCTION

To journey without being changed is to be a nomad.
To change without journeying is to be a chameleon.
To journey and be transformed by the journey is to be a pilgrim.[1]

Mark Nepo

Our society is hyperfocused on telling people how to be successful. And we embrace this. After all, most of us live with a degree of certainty and spend our time tweaking our lives, making each day a bit better than the one before. So often people say that their goal in life is to "just be a good person." Interpreted, this often means low-risk, safe, incremental living. Another day, another dollar. We hope our health will hold out a little longer, so we take a few more vitamins. We know we should "work on our marriage," so we pick up a magazine or peruse a blog for some helpful hints. We pray that our kids will avoid drugs and won't get their girlfriends pregnant.

Because the pursuit of a safe, comfortable, and controlled life is so central to our Western existence, we're often surprised, even angered, when we discover that our well-planned future has not provided the satisfaction and joy we were hoping for. Worse yet, we feel stuck, unmotivated, and frustrated. It seems that despite our best efforts, we have lost our joy and sense of purpose.

Life, once an adventure, is now a burden.

Stuck, unsure, and without direction, we live out a masquerade, hoping desperately that someone will love us and accept us when we pull the mask off.

Until we tell the story of the mask, we will never take it off.

Until we find someone who is fully present, who listens to understand, we will keep hiding.

When we tell our stories, and when we are truly heard, we begin to clean out the compost of our souls. We then begin a journey of subtraction. We courageously begin to take off the emotional armor that we have collected until we can find childlike wonder again.

A return to innocence.

A longing for Eden.

A quest that is never fully realized on this side of heaven.

A journey that cannot be ignored.

The exploration of genuine relationships, the self-discovery, the emergence of mystery, and a willingness to get lost and found in Truth compels us to go.

I am not an expert. I am but a pilgrim.

My great desire is to encourage you to know and be known, to experience a deep well of love and to give that love away. I have learned a few things that have helped me get unstuck. A unique adventure is ahead, and my hope is that what follows will guide you into a life full of passion and freedom—a life lived unrehearsed and unstuck.

There are twelve principles, or "prompts," that follow.

They are a pilgrim's attempt at wisdom.

Please don't turn them into a formula. That would miss the point.

Use them as prompts. Allow them to refresh your memory and remind you that you do not have to remain stuck.

A book is always a journey. My hope is that in the exchange of writing, reading, and reflecting, we can voyage together. My deep desire is that the tone of this book is not one of proving that I am right. My hope is that in my story and in my brokenness and in my redemption, Truth might be revealed.

There is an abundant life before us. We cannot find it on our own. We are meant to share this story we find ourselves in. You are not alone. Someone is waiting for you ...

Chapter 1

NUMB

There is more in us than we know. If we can be
made to see it, perhaps, for the rest of our lives
we will be unwilling to settle for less.

Kurt Hahn

The tragedy of life is what dies inside a man while he lives.

Albert Schweitzer

A skeptic who distrusts relationships.
A preacher with a broken marriage.
A rock star who lost his voice.

An unusual combination for a vacation to Israel.

I had always wanted to go to Jerusalem. See the city that stands at the crossroads of history. With my marriage crumbling, the trip now seemed less about a discovery of history and more a discovery of soul.

No longer a trip. A pilgrimage.

I was going with two friends: Josh, a skeptic who questioned the existence of God, and my friend Mark, a rock star who had lost his marriage and his voice. Mark had remarried, but his voice never came back. After seventeen years of touring, he was on a search for what was next.

THE END IS NEAR

It was cold that January morning of 2009. I was digging through my suitcase, packing my things. While checking my toiletry bag, I removed a container. The top fell off and hit the ground with an echoing clink.

My wife's wedding rings.

Angie had purposely placed them there for me to discover on the other side of the world.

The previous night we had had a blowout. I thought it had been just another familiar round of miscommunication. I hardly knew what to think anymore.

My heart dropped and my mind raced as I stood there holding the symbols of our eternal covenant. Her engagement
ring in particular had always been special. In my teens, I
discovered a handful of my father's baseball cards while
exploring my grandmother's attic. One lay facedown on
the floor. A 1956 Mickey Mantle. With little argument from
my father, I claimed the cards as my own and stored them
away.

I was a senior in college when I decided to propose to Angie.
I had no money but a little bit of stock and those baseball
cards. What could be a better reason to cash it all in? I drove
to Hofert's Jewelers and bought her the ring. The ring now
lying in the palm of my hand.

I looked at the shiny band and its sparkling diamond and
then at myself in the mirror.

I felt numb.

I've since learned that you cannot selectively numb.

If you numb pain, you numb beauty.[1]

It's true. On that brisk January morning, my life was full of
blessing. Parents and sisters who loved me. Four beautiful
children. Wonderful friends. A job I loved. A trip to the Holy
Land ahead of me. A life that seemed to have significance.

It all had little meaning. I couldn't feel.

Anger had turned into a dull, pervasive ache. I didn't hate my wife. I wasn't even all that shocked at her gesture. She was full of anger, and there was little I could do anymore to manage it.

I stared at myself in the mirror, trying to see my soul.

The light was going out.

TIRED OF THE TENSION

Have you been there? Wondering, "What's the point?" Asking if you have the stamina to go on?

My son Jordan plays the guitar. I watch him often reach up to change the tension on the strings. Why? Without the proper tension, one cannot experience beautiful music, harmonious melodies, compositions that stir the heart, the soul.

God is repeatedly tuning our lives.

Many of us, however, are stuck. Tired of the tension, we have numbed ourselves. We have not been taught how to live in a state of contradictions. We hide. We stare. We plod along, wondering about it all.

All the while, God is tuning.

We are unaware. While shutting out pain, we abandoned listening to the music. The beauty dances nearby, but we only see darkness. We are asleep.

> Spirituality means waking up. Most people, even though they don't know it, are asleep. They're born asleep, they live asleep, they marry in their sleep, they breed children in their sleep, they die in their sleep.... People don't really want to be cured. What they want is relief; a cure is painful. Waking up is unpleasant.... [It's] comfortable in bed. It's irritating to be woken up.[2]

EMPTY INSIDE

In college I once saw a poster that said, "Life should be gulped and not sipped."

When we exit the simplicity of childhood, we begin the complexity of adolescence and adulthood with the tools given to us by our families and culture. With the independence we crave, we start accumulating.

We accrue triumphs and failures in academics, athletics, the arts, finances, and relationships. We learn. We grow. We consider. We second-guess. We crash forward. We fall back.

Life.

At times we see it for the adventure that it is. We gulp it. We embrace the tension. We live fully in the unknown.

At other times, we get timid and shy. We discover that control can be a useful tool to manage our circumstances and get from others what we need. Comfort, power, and approval become dominant forces and seem to woo us. When we cave to their calling, however, we are always left empty.

The Great Romance seeps away.

"Indeed, the many forces driving modern life have not only assaulted the life of our heart, they have also dismantled the heart's habitat—that geography of mystery and transcendence we knew so well as children."[3]

We are left holding the cup of life, content only to sip because we are afraid that what little is left will soon evaporate.

Anxiety rushes in like a flood. Hurt and shame move in as neighbors. Freedom is replaced by bondage.

We are controlled by the illusion of control. We stop feeling. We wonder when there will be nothing left inside.

My dear friends David and Leslie wrote these lyrics:

When the pieces seem too shattered
To gather off the floor
And all that seems to matter
Is that I don't feel You anymore
No, I don't feel You anymore

I need a reason to sing
I need a reason to sing
I need to know that You're still holding
The whole world in Your hands
I need a reason to sing

When I'm overcome by fear
And I hate everything I know
If this waiting lasts forever
I'm afraid I might let go
I'm afraid I might let go

I need a reason to sing
I need a reason to sing
I need to know that You're still holding
The whole world in Your hands
I need a reason to sing.[1]

This was me. I had stopped feeling.

You may know what that's like. Feelings that previously seemed important have vanished.

We used to care. Now we don't.

We used to fight. Not so much.

We used to get angry. Waste of energy.

Something inside is dying. That something is called hope.

QUEST FOR EDEN

A litany of suppressed and unidentified patterns of behavior in our sixteen years of marriage had stacked themselves in a corner for years. Visited but never fully explored. Over the past year the stack had fallen over, and Angie and I found ourselves in an absolute mess.

My determination to spend time with my skeptic and rock star friends became the catalyst for our nosedive. For Angie, this decision transported her to the pinnacle of her pain. It left her feeling rejected and abandoned.

Her story had shaped her in such a way that she craved attention. Being a firstborn and assuming this was a "love language" thing, I did everything I thought possible to supply what she needed. After years of emotional maneuvering, my tank emptied, and I found that I had little left to give.

I didn't have enough awareness to realize it at the time, but what I thought was unconditional love was simply pain management. I didn't want to hurt Angie or make her angry, so I capitulated regularly to her preferences and desires.

In her lack of awareness, she was hoping to get from me something I could never deliver. A fellow human could not meet her quest for satisfaction and closure. Only God could satisfy the longings that seemed to overtake her, and even then, the satisfaction would be momentary. I had my own issues to contend with. My inability to set boundaries and fear of disapproval were hindering our relationship. Unknowingly, we both were on a quest for Eden, and in this lifetime, Eden was not accessible.

The night before I left for Israel we had slammed into another disastrous moment of miscommunication. We were so far off the map, I had no idea what to say or do anymore. In Angie's fear, she felt rage. In my insecurity, I chose silence.

By morning, with no resolution, I was left with my wife's wedding rings and words of anger echoing in the chambers of my heart. I felt very alone. Disrupted. Disconnected.

> *We each are asked to make our way through the drama of our bleeding to the stripping of our will, through the tensions of our suffering to the humility of surrender where we might learn the ordinary art of living at the pace of what is real.*[5]
>
> Mark Nepo

RESISTANCE

Learning to feel again begins by opening ourselves. What we fear the most—being vulnerable—is what we have to become.

There is an ancient truth spoken by Jesus of Nazareth and recorded by a fisherman who followed Him: "The thief comes only to steal and kill and destroy; I have come that they may have life, and have it to the full."[6]

It seems there is a villain in our story. There are forces of evil that are hell-bent on stealing our joy, killing our relationships, and destroying any hope for connection. Steven Pressfield calls this villain *Resistance*:

> Resistance's goal is not to wound or disable. Resistance aims to kill. Its target is the epicenter of our being: our genius, our soul, the unique and priceless gift we were put on earth to give and that no one else has but us. Resistance means business. When we fight it, we are in a war to the death.[7]

When we strip the exterior of life away, what we are left with is connection. We have each been invited into a story about connection. The connection of God with His creation and the connection of mankind with God and with one another.

Our brokenness alienates us. Pushes us away from God and people. God's Spirit is always moving us toward reconciliation with Him and reconciliation with others.

Keep thy heart with all diligence; for out
of it are the issues of life.[8]

A Hebrew proverb

CONNECTION BREEDS HOPE

The pilgrimage in Israel was filled with extraordinary moments, important stories to be told on another day. As our adventure drew to a close, reality set in. I had trouble suppressing the disruption in my spirit. Passing on yet another falafel and munching on McDonald's french fries at a mall in Tel Aviv, I detonated the dam and let my anguish spill out over my friends.

Josh looked at me and said, "You look done."

"I'm not, but I feel that way," I responded.

Mark, who had been through remarkably similar patterns of codependency in his first marriage, listened for a long time before saying a word. "You can't give up hope," he admonished. "You have to believe. I know you hurt, but she does too. If there is a chance, you have to hold on to it."

As men, we made a few vain attempts to strategize how I should respond to Angie when I returned. But by the end, I dumped what I thought I knew on God and decided I must defer to His Spirit's guidance.

Redemption seemed to exist only in a galaxy far, far away, but these men had watered seeds of belief. Unknowingly, in my confession and vulnerability and their empathy and encouragement, a soul environment had emerged.

Our friendship had submerged to a different depth.

In my heart I was starting to feel something again. I felt genuinely connected to these men. I felt valued. As I left the table, my pain stayed with me, but my hurt now had a companion: hope.

I was beginning to understand something my friend Wayne often spoke of: "You can't heal what you don't acknowledge."

Denial is a coping mechanism. We choose denial because the pain we fear seems too great. And it might be. If you open Pandora's box, you may not be able to deal with what lies within. But from a certain perspective, that's the point.

Until we realize we are not our own sufficiency, we will remain feeling stuck and unloved.

WAKING UP

There is a battle for our souls that rages whether we are aware of it or not. Love is pulling us one way, and death and destruction another.

How do we shake ourselves from slumber?

How do we allow ourselves to feel when we know that pain awaits?

How do we get moving again?

There is a way. There is hope.

Wake up.

Acknowledge that something isn't right.

Something changes in the universe when you confess, admit, and declare truth. It seems that when you speak it out, truth is invited in.

I read somewhere that the first Catholic confessional was started by a priest who discovered that the poor he worked with needed a safe place to clean out their souls. When these folks finally put into words their sins and sufferings, they felt the heaviness of their lives fall away. They lifted their heads again and walked with a truer sense of purpose.

Whether you speak to a pastor, a priest, a family member, a friend, the mirror, or God Himself, speak. Say what you feel is wrong. Communicate your desire for life to be different. Take off your mask.

Lift up your head.
Feel the sun on your face.
Today is a new day.

Good morning. You're waking up.

  1. *Stuck? Say it. Acknowledge it. Open your eyes.*

Chapter 2

A RELUCTANT
NAVIGATOR

Every choice [is] ... a renunciation.[1]

Thomas Aquinas

*We live mainly by forms and patterns.... If
the forms are bad, we live badly.*[2]

Wallace Stegner

I worked with teenagers for thirteen years. The list of crazy activities I have been involved in seems endless.

One night at a retreat center near Fort Lauderdale, Florida, we decided to play an adventurous night game of capture the flag. As it was extremely dark that evening, we used flashlights as the "flag." The goal was to stealthily creep into the other team's territory, steal the flag, and return to your home base.

Being just a bit competitive in those days, I was highly focused on becoming the heroic capturer. I crept along the edge of the field unnoticed, waited for the right moment, leaped from my place of concealment, grabbed the flashlight, and sprinted at full speed toward the opposite side of the field.

I was unaware that the wall protecting the swimming pool had an unusual freestanding extension tapering off to about shin level. (Did I mention that I was competitive and sprinting at full speed?)

No one has ever hit me with a baseball bat at full swing across my legs, but I think I have a pretty good idea of what that would feel like.

I hit the wall so hard my shin immediately split open, and I flipped through the air and over the wall. It's important to note that I was also unaware that the random wall extending off the swimming pool had a six-foot drop on the other side of it.

I landed mostly on my throat.

My bleeding leg arrived afterward with the rest of my flailing body. My nervous system was apparently overloaded by the excitement, and I lay on the ground, shaking and twitching.

Fortunately, there were cheering teenagers nearby who felt like the registration fee for the retreat was now totally worth it.

With a degree of vibrato, I asked for help, and before long I was given a neck brace, strapped to a gurney, and taken on a drug-induced ambulance joy ride.

Thankfully, all was well. Save for some missing bone and an absence of feeling on my shin. Doctors sewed me up, and other than a small indention, my leg healed fine. To this day, the skin on the center of my shin is numb. If you put a pin up to it, I feel no pain.

I have a sneaking suspicion, however, that if I were to sprint into my favorite wall again, I would feel something. Pain would emanate from a deeper place.

I think our hearts function in a similar way. When we say we feel numb, we imply we don't feel anything. Of course we feel *something*. The question is, *what* am I feeling, and how deep is that feeling buried?

A FRAGMENTING MARRIAGE

The first seven years of our marriage were good. A couple of job changes, the birth of twin boys, the purchase of our first home—fairly uneventful as far as major catastrophes go. However, during the delivery of our third child, Angie had complications, and as a result, she received two blood trans-fusions. Over time her hormones failed to balance out. Angie shares that this, combined with her inability to lose weight and the challenges she felt parenting three children under three, caused her sense of worth to plummet and seemed to awaken our latent dysfunction from its hibernation.

Over the next ten years nothing ever seemed to be enough for Angie.

She felt this pressure to constantly improve. She had a keen ability to recognize what wasn't working in her life, other rela-tionships, and our marriage. The eye of the critic was both a blessing and a curse.

Angie was an avid reader and tenacious in her desire to be a better person and for us to have a better marriage. This has always been one of the traits I've admired about her. She would discover later, however, that much of this came from an unrelenting determination to be seen and known. When I was not attentive, she interpreted my actions as rejection.

I was a performer. I grew up acting, singing, storytelling, and searching for approval. I was also taught that I was to love unconditionally and live a life dedicated to saving people. A professor of mine in college once told me, "It is always your turn." So I lived, believing and behaving as if it was "always my turn."

With my proclivity and training, I did my best to meet each of Angie's expectations. As the years progressed, I couldn't keep up. Her expectations became more demanding and her anger more intense when those expectations weren't met. My father, who has been a teacher, counselor, and pastor for many years, has reminded us that in many ways another term for anger is *blocked goals*. This seemed to be the perfect definition for what we struggled with. When each of our expectations was not met, the temperature of passionate expression would rise.

I started acting not out of love, but out of duty. As I said—acting.

In time, focusing on managing my wife's demands, I began losing all sense of self. In deferring my preferences, I was also deferring my responsibility. I didn't know it at the time, but I was inept at setting healthy boundaries. I wasn't helping our marriage but accelerating its downward spiral.

We were both wearing thin.

In the midst of this marital unrest, however, God remained faithful. Often, it seemed He was unaffected by our inability to thrive as a married couple. Which was a little frustrating because I wanted Him to be more bothered about the whole thing.

But rather than removing the tension, He seemed to be preparing to remove us.

ANYTHING BUT A PASTOR

It started as a whisper.

If I am completely honest, the whisper had been there for a long time. Maybe even for a decade. But as time progressed, the volume increased.

A voice. Telling me it was time to pastor a church. I resisted. I remember thinking, *No way. I have known too many pastors. I don't belong in that tribe*.

I suppose most of us look at life through the lens of our experience. I am no exception. I never wanted to become a pastor because of what I thought that meant. From my perspective, it meant wearing a suit—frequently—and being unapproachable. Aloof. And right about everything.

I don't know that I could have articulated it then, but the primary reason I didn't want to become a pastor was because I didn't want to become distant. Onstage I often saw pastors with furrowed brows, frustrated with sinners and their sin. Off the stage,

I experienced most pastors as being preoccupied, inauthentic, controlling, and, well, unkind. Not to say that their lives were lived out that way, but these were my lasting impressions.

Somewhere along the way I took a personality test called the DiSC profile. It explains that there are four different types of personalities:

- D's are Decisive. They are often aggressive and competitive. They prefer problem solving and getting results.
- I's are Interactive. They are often enthusiastic and persuasive. They prefer spending time with others and showing emotion.
- S's are Stabilizing. They are often patient and predictable. They prefer pacing, steadiness, and persistence.
- C's are Cautious. They are often analytical and perfectionistic. They prefer procedures, standards, and protocols.

Without restraint, D's have no hesitation functioning as God in His apparent absence. D's have a purpose and a plan for your life. And if you or God do not tell them otherwise, they will work hard to fulfill the plan they have for you.

From what I could tell, throughout my young life, my spiritual leaders wanted me to function as a D. So I was trained that way.

One of the hallmarks of my training was the art of selling. My friend Ron calls it "Point of Sale Evangelism." The goal of every interaction with a human being was to "win their soul" or "get them saved."

The Soul Winner would initiate a conversation by asking, "If you were to die tonight, where would you go?" This was a scare tactic for getting the person motivated to avoid hell and acquire heaven through a "simple prayer." A prayer that apparently summed up all of the mystery of God and His relationship with humanity.

If one wanted to double-check one's work—to see if the conversion worked or was genuine—one could follow up with the customer to see if they meant it "with all their heart." The Soul Winner would then report this salvation decision to church leadership or denominational headquarters. Somewhere it would be recorded that one more soul had been saved from hell and was now on its way to heaven, as if that were the primary reason for one's existence.

Taking the time to know someone, to climb around in that person's story, to bear the tension of struggles and questions, was optional at best.

Considering what I learned in the DiSC profile, this kind of evangelism is a great plan for D's.

They thrive on problem solving: lost person now saved.

They love competition and, in particular, winning. There is no higher moral calling than winning a soul.

They are driven toward success: the higher the number of "saved" people, the more accolades they receive.

They feel safest when they are in control: lost person discovers that they are wrong and the D was right, and now they must follow the teachings of the aforementioned D in order to spiritually grow.

Selling people on Jesus and offering them a get-out-of-hell-free card through the medium of a prayer cliché, however unintentional, is the message I was taught from childhood. I was told repeatedly that I could know, beyond the shadow of a doubt, that I was bound for heavenly bliss if I was confident in this great, prayerful transaction.

> *Salvation is not a prayer you pray in a one-time ceremony and then move on from; salvation is a posture of repentance and faith that you begin in a moment and maintain for the rest of your life.*[3]
>
> J. D. Greear

The great irony was that many of those same religious instructors were saying there was no moral act or behavior that could save you. I lived confused and continually unsettled, even as powerful communicators shamed me for my lack of courage to confront people daily with the truth that they were sinners bound for hell. The whole process never sat right with me. It seemed shallow and empty, missing something. This compulsion is what drove me to explore a deeper understanding of God and His kingdom.

I was told by my spiritual leaders that it was a bummer for people like Mother Teresa.

She had dedicated her entire life to serving the "least of these,"[4] the widowed, the poor, the orphaned.[5] She had ignored material wealth and spent daily time with Jesus in the Bible and in prayer. But because she didn't pray a certain prayer in a certain way, hell was all that awaited her.

> *Religion is lived by people who are afraid of hell. Spirituality*
> *is lived by people who have been through hell.*[6]
>
> Richard Rohr

Darren, one of the leaders in our church, had been a very successful music manager for many years when he felt like God was calling him to leave his career and start a new church. We celebrated his faith and sent him off to pour out his heart into the needs of others. One day we were talking about our strengths and inadequacies, asking somewhat rhetorically why God chose us to be pastors. After thinking about the changes in our culture and reflecting on the many conversations I had enjoyed with other spiritual explorers, I sent this email off to Darren:

> I wonder if D's were successful in culture past because ours was a culture (think trickle-down puritanism) in which shaming was accepted ... even considered a useful form of motivation. Maybe the days of large enterprising churches are waning, as D's are no longer given the luxury of treating people as less than human. Maybe culture, combined with the movement of the Spirit, has thrown "authenticity" to the forefront as saints have prayed away the principality of hierarchal, power-over Christianity.

> Maybe this is a season for the I's and S's. So maybe God uses us ... with our approval issues, lack of training, trouble with boundaries ... and wouldn't it be interesting if that is why we are serving in [Nashville,] an ethos-shaping town ... maybe it's like turn-of-the-century California, believing there is gold but knowing the odds are stacked against us. Maybe the courage to go will supersede the inadequacies that linger ... "Being confident of this, that he who began a good work in [us] will carry it on to completion until the day of Christ Jesus."[7]

I am not saying all D's are bad. I hope not, as I have some in me. And we do desperately need mature versions of that personality type. Clearly God uses them. They are decisive and daring. It seems they are often the ones guiding organizations and inciting movements. I just wonder if our culture is becoming less tolerant of a personality type that when bent in dysfunction veers toward abuse.

Whatever the personality trait, why is it that so many are driven toward certainty and measured success? Is it God-induced passion or self-induced shame? Does the quest for certainty produce within us a pleasant trust or an anxious fear?

FAITH AND UNCERTAINTY

I forever have had trouble fitting in with religious people, the type who have certain ways of doing things. The word *certain* is very important to them because being right is possibly the central value of their life construct.

I was always uncertain about their certainty. I think this made them feel uncomfortable. Uncomfortable religious people who cannot get someone to conform to their way of certainty and submit to their mechanisms of control become insecure religious people.

In their insecurity they dehumanize. They demonstrate their gift for branding. They label and categorize others in an attempt to defend their castle of specificity. Ambiguity is always the enemy.

Questions about faith not fully resolved leave this type of religious person unsettled. Without moral certitude and authority they feel unsafe. Exposed. Vulnerable. Out of control. If they do not have an answer for you, which is rare, they will hustle off to their books to find one. They will study and read until they have applied enough logic and reason to maintain a strong position on whatever it is you questioned them about.

All of this carries with it a certain degree of irony, as religious people tend to describe themselves as people of faith. The cornerstone verse used for faith is found in Hebrews, a book in the Bible: "Now faith is the substance of things hoped for, the evidence of things not seen."[8] And as author Jeremy Young observes, "A claim to possess certainty is an illegitimate attempt to deny human limitations and is also, in essence, *an attempt to live without faith.*"[9]

To truly live by faith, one must be willing to live in the tension of not knowing. Not understanding certain things. Not having all the answers. A person must walk humbly, bearing the mystery of a God who far surpasses any human capacity to fully define Him.

Religious zealots resist this. At a subconscious level I believe it's because they resist a relationship that cannot be distilled into a formula. But what they really resist is emotional closeness. They are afraid of being deeply loved. Thus, they find security and distance in distinction.

I have learned something about labels. Inhuman words that are used to describe humans purposely distance humans from their humanness. When we call someone a tool, a wacko, a nut job, a moron, a freak, a neutralized target, a Baptist, a Catholic, a liberal, a conservative, an ethnic slur, and so on, we remove their humanity. And with it their divine spark.

A divine image bearer is more than a number or a notch on a belt. A person represents a very specific and unique design by the God of the universe to imprint the world.

You and I are stories and carry within us, whether we are aware of it or not, *the* Story.

THE SHADOW SIDE

My struggle with becoming a pastor was ultimately a trust problem. I didn't trust myself.

And I liked approval. I tried not to, but people's perceptions of me were always more important than I wanted them to be.

The idea of being a pastor made me nauseous. Nauseous because the title struck fear that I might become the very thing I had for so long resisted.

I did not want to be driven by ego.
I did not want to humiliate and shame others out of my jealousy.

I did not want to be narrow-minded.

I did not want to be closed off from people, hiding my darkest secrets.

I did not want to be perpetually frustrated with those who disagreed with me.

I genuinely loved God. And I genuinely loved people (teenagers in particular because they seemed less pretentious and in general pretty honest). But there was this shadow side. I was constantly trying to prove myself.

I was stuck.

To ignore what I was sensing, a call to start and pastor a new church, would be a heart betrayal and a disobedience to what I genuinely believed the Author was writing in me. To move forward was to risk being labeled and misperceived. To move forward was to risk becoming like the people who hurt me.

It's exhausting trying to manage the future, isn't it?

CLIFF DIVING

I wonder if all of life is lived at the edge of a cliff.

We either leap in faith or get kicked off in complacency. We either jump off believing we will fly, or we get knocked off, flailing and screaming about how we don't like change.

Want to get unstuck? Get moving again.

Get out of bed. Take a step. Write something. Pray something. Go to the gym and lift something.

We do not just drift into becoming the best version of ourselves.[10]

John Ortberg

Move forward. We must not let fear or shame pin us to the ground. A decision to take a step is what the Bible refers to as faith. Faith is stepping into the unknown. Faith equals movement.

God calls and empowers us from a place of motion. And "if you wait for guarantees, the only thing that will be guaranteed is that you will miss endless divine opportunities."[11]

Sometimes we wander around, looking for the God-designed life.

Sometimes we sit around, waiting for our purpose to find us.

> Go to the ant, O sluggard, observe her ways and be wise.[12]

What if we faithfully engaged the needs of the day?

What if we were intentional with our solitude?

What if we were to step into something new?

Angie and I jumped off the cliff the summer of 2005. After eight years of working with students near Saint Louis, Missouri, we left a two-million-dollar youth facility that we had labored to design and build, an amazing team of leaders, and five hundred teenagers who inspired us in their exploration of faith. In our lack of awareness, our marital dysfunction, and our struggle with identity, God still loved us and used us to love others. We still heard His voice, and in our hearts we deeply desired to obey Him.

After receiving counsel and much prayer, we surrendered to what felt like an imperative from God. Emboldened by the mission to find what we didn't know, we would start a church for those disenfranchised *with* the church. Convinced that God was leading us, we moved to Nashville, Tennessee.

1. Stuck? Say it. Acknowledge it. Open your eyes.

2. Stuck? Do something new. Find resistance and push through it.

Chapter 3

PUT ASIDE THE RANGER

Modern man [is] plagued by distractions, addictions,
obsessions, never at home in his own skin, never truly
connecting with others, never at one with present reality,
and anxiously awaiting a plane going nowhere.[1]

Mike Mason

The imagination should be allowed a certain
freedom to browse around.[2]

Thomas Merton

"This past Friday I checked myself into a hotel. I had a number of drinks, took eleven pills, and told God I was done. If I woke up the next morning, then I would talk to someone about why I am still here." This thirtysomething, well-to-do soccer mom confessed that she was without hope.

"She wants a divorce. I don't want one. I am just waking up, beginning to feel for the first time in my life. But I don't think it matters. She has felt so lost for so long that regardless of our three children she wants out. I am afraid there is not much hope." My friend, a very successful British musician, was desperate.

"My husband and I have been in this oppressive religious system for so long, I feel like I have lost my soul. He is loyal and has tried to do everything in his power to adjust to the ridiculous demands of our leadership. His spirit is crushed. I am angry and not sure how much more of this I can take." My friend and her husband were missionaries who were holding their lives together by tattered spiritual threads.

IDENTITY LOST

I have spent many years listening to people's stories. My heart has always leaned toward those grasping tightly to hope.

They are without pretense.

They are not trying to sell you something.

They are not obsessed with being right (on the contrary, they usually hope they are wrong).

They are awake.

They are aware of pain.

Suffering has forced them on a quest.

They are looking for something or someone.

They are teachable.

They are grateful.

I have learned something about coming to the end of your rope.

You fall in terror until you crash, or you fall in exhilaration until you fly.

At a conscious and unconscious level, we choose between fear and faith each and every moment of our day. Why? Because no matter how much we structure our lives and build in layers of control, we cannot shake the reality of the unknown.

When life's circumstances make us acutely aware of its chaotic churning, we often choose to numb ourselves, to temporarily relieve pressure.

We cut.

We self-loathe.

We punish ourselves to remind us that we are real, all the while gouging out our souls. We forget who we were and who we were made to become.

J. R. R. Tolkien extraordinarily captures this tension in his character Aragorn from the Lord of the Rings trilogy.

Aragorn's father, the only descendent of a long-dead king, dies in battle. Aragorn's mother takes the two-year-old boy to be raised by Lord Elrond and the Elves. When Aragorn comes of age, he learns that he is the rightful heir to the throne of the world of men.

But Aragorn has watched men. They are crude and vengeful, untrustworthy. He fears the blood that runs through his veins. He is anxious that were he to lead, he would become just like them.

He resists his destiny. Aragorn lives under an alias, content to fight trivial skirmishes in far-off lands. Eventually, fate thrusts him into the center of the world of men. One day, with the freedom of Middle Earth hanging in the balance, his mentor Lord Elrond visits him.

Lord Elrond uncloaks the sword of the ancient king and gives it to Aragorn with this charge: "Put aside the ranger. Become who you were born to be."[3]

AWAKENING

Our first three months on the ground in Nashville became a sort of purge. Our previous church experience and a hurried schedule consumed by programming had run us hard. When it all went away, the discontentment that was a part of catapulting us into this church-planting adventure only escalated.

In the longing and questioning, we were learning.

A couple of things became clear early on. We yearned for authentic relationships, and we understood that they would not happen overnight. A relationship of depth cannot be found in a formula. A soul environment requires risk, vulnerability, listening, slowing.

While we didn't know much, we were confident about one thing: we did not want FDA-approved, assembly-line relationships that were predictably safe and discarded when broken.

And so, my wife and I and the adventurers we collected along the way got honest and vulnerable. As we shared our own stories and entered the stories of others, we discovered the souls of people. No longer seen first in color, level of couth, or denomination, but seen first as image bearers of God, containers of something eternal.

My sister Jineen and brother-in-law Shane; Allie, a freshman at Belmont; three friends from college; a nurse; a furniture saleswoman; a girl we had met at the pool; a magician and his wife from down the road; and our real-estate agent gathered in our living room, and we called it a church.

In time this experience changed me.

It affected the way I looked at success.

I rejected my training of focusing on numerical measurement.

I found joy in living life alongside broken people.

It is only by risking ourselves from one hour
to another that we live at all.[4]

William James

Jesus was loving people through me. In return, I encountered Jesus' love. The more I served, the more I experienced new rhythms of life. I started leading less and listening more.

Rather than selling people on a vision that would make their lives better, I looked for ways to guide people into what God was designing for them.

I found myself identifying with others as they told me their stories of brokenness and longing. I was making deep connections with people. Real people. The emotions that I shoved to the recesses of my heart were suddenly validated. I wasn't the only one who struggled with questions and uncertainty.

This was exhilarating. But also very revealing. Ignorance is only bliss temporarily. Eventually life caves in and the denial that one lives in must be acknowledged.

The love of God, as Angie and I began to experience it more intensely, spotlighted a contrast. We did not love each other well. We were beginning to realize how much we had settled. Angie's attempt at connection took the form of a commodity exchange. Mine was steeped in duty.

By now, Angie's desire to be seen and known had subtly become an addiction. She became easily frustrated when she wasn't getting the attention she desired from me. The self-help books, which were her confidence and formula for living, weren't working.

I lived in denial. I didn't know how to give Angie what she needed, and I lived under the illusion that if I kept trying, eventually I could make her happy.

We both were in pain but in different ways. It was freeing for me to know that other people had the same struggles, but it was burdensome as well. I could no longer deny the reality of the pain and heartache I felt each day.

NOW WHAT?

Our families are shaped by the behaviors, decisions, and actions of previous generations. There is no perfect family. And there are no perfect people. The raw reality of our brokenness is a harsh truth.

When we become aware of the patterns that we have followed and the habits we have acquired, a question naturally follows: "What are we going to do about it?"

The usual response is to figure out a way to escape the tension as quickly as possible. We pray for a miracle. We hunt down a secret formula. We listen to a talk-show host. We download a podcast. Nothing wrong with any of this—it's just that we are rarely given the escape that we so long for.

Developing healthy patterns of relating takes emotional energy.

Fostering balanced relationships takes time.

The terms *emotional energy* and *time* used alongside each other makes most men want to sprint in the other direction.

Most men just want the problem fixed. They don't want to talk it out, and they don't want to listen it out either. If they ignore it long enough, maybe it will just go away or fix itself.

Denial was a drug of choice for me. Each morning I would wake up as if my life was a part of the opening theme to the *Mary Tyler Moore Show*. I would stretch my arms, embrace denial, and think, *Today it will all change for the better, Jamie. You're gonna make it after all.*

But realizing that all is not well, that things are not right, that we feel disconnected from the ones we love or the One we love is like walking into a clearing in a forest. Everything stops looking the same, and we gain a new orientation. We notice the location of the sun. Finding or creating this space gives us room and time to recollect ourselves.

> *Harassed by life, exhausted, we look about us for somewhere to be quiet, to be genuine, a place of refreshment. We yearn to restore our spirits in God.*[5]
>
> Hans Urs von Balthasar

Here's what I mean. What if you had to read the previous few paragraphs like this?

Theusualresponseistofigureoutawaytoescapethetensionas-quicklyaspossibleWeprayforamiracleWehuntdownasecretfor-mulaWelistentoatalkshowhostWedownloadapodcastNothingw-rongwithanyofthisit'sjustthatwearerarelygiventheescapethatwe solongforDevelopinghealthypatternsofrelatingtakesemotionale-nergyFosteringbalancedrelationshipstakestimeThetermsemo-tionalenergyandtimeusedalongsideeachothermakesmostmen-

wanttosprintintheotherdirectionMostmenjustwanttheproblem-
fixed.Theydon'twanttotalkitoutandtheydon'twanttolistenitoutei
therIftheyignoreitlongenoughmaybeitwilljustgoawayorfixitself.

We don't print books this way because we know that the brain needs space to process. If we had to read like this all the time, it would be frustrating, exhausting, and, for most of us, stressful!

Yet it is interesting that many of us tend to live our lives without space.

This was true for Angie and me.

I was hurt and angry at Angie's excessive demands. I would raise my voice, thinking somehow that changing the volume would shut off the emotional vacuum I felt was aimed at me. I sighed. I turned my back. I went quiet. But nothing worked. I projected anger toward my wife, but the truth was I was angry with myself. Why was I unable to resist the pressure I felt to conform to Angie's ideals? I felt like a dog on a leash.

Compelled by duty, I would sit for hours at a time and listen to her latest analysis of our marriage and why it wasn't working and the steps we had to take to make it better.

One time I asked if, for a change of pace, we could take one evening and just celebrate what *was* going right. From her perspective there was no room for that. There was too much that had to change. The books that she read fed her obsession about creating the perfect marriage, and I was ill equipped to counter her aggressive criticism.

Sitting with our marriage counselor, Doyle, I asked him what my problem was. Why couldn't I control the way I was feeling? We had met several times by this point, and he sensed it was time to really drive home a point. Like a boxer who had his opponent on the ropes, he knew it was time for the knockout punch and unloaded: "Well, your problem is you are a [expletive] coward."

Being called a coward did not produce in me immediate feelings of affection or appreciation. I thought to myself, *I just paid him to call me a [expletive] coward. Apparently I am also a [expletive] masochist.*

I didn't like the way that sounded, but he was right. I had within me a deep fear of disapproval, and it prevented me from loving Angie from a place of strength.

WHY SPACE MATTERS

Spaces in a sentence allow room for understanding. They give us perspective so that we can see parts and connect them to the whole. Sometimes we even get double spaces between sentences to give us a moment to pause and collect ourselves, letting the previous thought land and creating room for the next one to take flight.

There is a story about an old rabbi and a young Jewish man. The rabbi saw the young man running very quickly.

Rabbi: What are you doing?

Young man: I am running to make my living.

Rabbi: But perhaps in the process you are losing your life.[6]

> *[People] intoxicate themselves with work so*
> *they won't see how they really are.*
> Aldous Huxley

We must intentionally slow things down. We must learn how to actively wait. "When you wait, you are not doing nothing. You're doing the most important something there is. You're allowing your soul to grow up."[7]

> *[Waiting] calls us to be in this moment, this season, without leaning*
> *so far into the future that we tear our roots from the present.*[8]
> Sue Monk Kidd

Whether or not we realize this, we subconsciously create buffer zones.

Our minds recognize we need the space.

Think about it.

Has there been a time when you actually looked forward to the drive home? No one around. Maybe you even turned the radio off. You knew you needed silence. Space.

Or maybe after dinner you go for a walk. You intuitively know that along with providing exercise for the body, space is restful for the soul.

The mind that comes to rest is tended
In ways that it cannot intend:
Is borne, preserved, and comprehended
By what it cannot comprehend.[9]

Wendell Berry

SHOW ME SOMETHING

In January of 2009, in the center of my pain and my darkest hour, I found myself with a skeptic and a rock star in the land where Jesus walked. I was acutely aware of my need for Him. I was out of answers. And an old, familiar feeling of rejection was creeping back up on me. Something I was quite familiar with from my middle school years.

Angie, meanwhile, had driven to Alabama to stay with her family. Her formulas were not working, and those abandoned rings she'd left in my bag were a last-ditch effort at getting my attention.

We both felt a deep and fierce loneliness.

My friends and I spent the first few days in Jerusalem, then we moved on to Galilee. I longed for something to take away my pain.

I needed space. I had to believe that my pain would be assuaged in this place.

This was where Jesus had grown up! I wanted Him to carry me like the old poem my parents had hanging in their house. So one morning I got up early and went to the beach, looking for the "footprints." This is a page from my journal that day:

> *Sunrise. The Sea of Galilee. The wind is crisp as I sit with my Bible in my lap, browsing through stories that cling to the air all around me. I am sitting on a ledge overlooking the beach. Somewhere along this shoreline, Jesus had breakfast with His friends. In just a little while, I will have breakfast with mine.*

> *Yesterday, Shimone, our tour guide, had arranged a private boat ride out into the middle of Galilee's sea. The water was smooth and the lake was quiet; it seemed hesitant to reveal its ageless mystery.*

> *In an impulsive, testosterone-lined moment, Mark stripped down to his briefs and jumped into the*

chilly January water. It didn't take much persua-sion for Josh and me to follow.

The sailors were clearly amused by the pasty Gentile morons who leaped from their perfectly good boat. We paddled for a few seconds, climbed back on board, did a pose-off for the camera, and laughed and made fun of one another while we sun dried.

Remembering those moments from yesterday, I thought about Jesus and His disciples. They were guys. They burped, gassed, annoyed one another, shoved Judas into the water (well, he seemed kind of stiff, so I would have). They were just guys figuring out life together.

While I am grateful for these friendships, for the fun we have had, and for the memories we have made, I find myself wanting more.

I want to hang out with You, Jesus.

Here am I, Lord.

I have traveled across the globe to visit the land You inhabited.

You walked on this beach. You shut down a storm
in this very place.

You walked out on that water! Why am I not feeling
You more?!

I spent the better part of an hour pleading for God's presence to overwhelm me.

Nada. Nothing. If anything, I felt isolated and distant.

No matter what I tried, I sat there. Emotionless.

Finally, I left and joined the guys for breakfast. I looked across the table at Josh and said, "I saw the sunrise this morning. I went out to the sea to meet with God."

Josh tilted his head and raised his eyebrows, awaiting my revelation.

"Yeah. He didn't show," I murmured.

My skeptic friend took a bite of his scrambled eggs, thought for a moment, and said, "Maybe He wants you to stay in your discomfort a little longer? Maybe there is no immediate rescue plan?"

Ironic. That was the first time I had heard from God all morning.

We drove from Galilee to Nazareth later that morning and upon arrival entered the Saint Gabriel Hotel. We sat down to refreshments with the hotel's owners, two sisters. They were Arab-Israeli Christian businesswomen. In Nazareth, you would call that being in a minority. They were very sharp ladies who had been educated abroad and spent much of their time involved in international business.

My friend Robert thought it might be a good idea for us to meet. After brief introductions and a short recounting of our experiences in their country, they began to speak passionately of their desire for their city to discover that redemption could be found only in Jesus. They shared with us the difficulty and loneliness of dwelling in the margins of a storied city whose resounding center was the child-God who once played in its streets.

The younger sister spoke fervently about her desire to serve the impoverished and disadvantaged of Nazareth. She shared specifically about her desire to start an orphanage. The older sister, with deep emotion yet remarkable poise, described the teenagers who swarmed the city streets. She talked of their love for music and their intense search for truth. She quoted Jesus, saying, "The harvest is plentiful, but the workers are few."

I told them their vision was beautiful and inspiring. Sensing their plea for help, I said that I could at the very least pray for them. I couldn't offer much more. I was a pastor, yes, but a broken one.

After what had felt like endless attempts to find equilibrium, I was the guy with his wife's wedding rings. Our relationship felt like a teenager learning to drive with a clutch. I had questions about whether I would be able to serve my own church, let alone others across the ocean.

REVELATION

As I finished my prayer, the women seemed grateful and unaffected by my self-indictment. They simply launched into further dialogue regarding their concern for their city. The older sister shared that she had asked God where she should go for direction regarding their vision. She said that He had told her that they were to go nowhere, that the men who could help them implement their vision would come to them. These men would find them in their hotel and would become their answer to prayer.

She looked around at the group and, resting her eyes on me, said with a confidence I have rarely known, "Jamie, while you were praying, God spoke again. You are the men we have been waiting for."

I couldn't speak. I pulled my hat lower and set my jaw, but I could not hold back my tears. They were spilling out and dripping off my chin, uninterested in my attempt at composure. Without saying it, she was saying, "This story is much bigger than your self-pity. Like it or not, God is going to use you."

I could not deny what was happening in my soul.

I had found God.

Or better, God was revealing Himself to me. Not on an ancient beach as I had presupposed, but among His children.

He wasn't finished with me. No matter how broken I was, He was not giving up. On the contrary, my pain seemed to be just what He had in mind.

Sitting in a hotel lobby, an unplanned and unexpected introduction to two foreign women opened my heart and my eyes to the presence of God. I don't think we ever get to predict connection. Sometimes it happens, and sometimes it doesn't.

I learned an important lesson, however, about how to make myself more available and aware when opportunity is close by. Watered in truth, connection blooms in the soil of vulnerability.

The Jewish people have a way of creating space. They do this every week and have for generations. It is called Sabbath. One day a week they are not productive. They cease working. They follow the example of God at creation.

> Thus the heavens and the earth were completed
> in all their vast array. By the seventh day God had

finished the work he had been doing; so on the seventh day he rested from all his work."[10]

God models for us the importance of bringing life to a halt and resting.

"Why is it so important to be finished? Perhaps because every unfinished task—from household chores to building a house, from someone we need to forgive to someone we need to remind we love—demands a piece of our attention. Such a task coaxes us to be back in yesterday, worrying about what we didn't finish, or it wants us to be already in tomorrow, worrying about what we still need to do. And whenever we are back in yesterday or already in tomorrow, we are not fully here. Our bodies are obviously present, but our attention is somewhere else."[11]

Sabbath is the key to essence and not mere existence.
Rabbi Riskin

"If there is no sabbath—no regular and commanded not-working, not-talking—we soon become totally absorbed in what we are doing and saying, and God's work is either forgotten or marginalized.... Un-sabbathed, our work becomes the entire context in which we define our lives."[12]

A couple of years ago I found a park that had a handful of isolated cabins in the woods. I rented one and spent four days there. With the exception of eating and sleeping, for the first two days all I did was sit on the porch and look out at the view or sit inside the cabin and stare at the walls. I did not restrain my mind but rather allowed it to empty itself. I thought about our church, my marriage, chocolate-chip cookies, Jack Bauer—whatever was on my mind I let the thoughts run until they ran out of steam. Finally, without having to fight off my brain, I felt I was ready to engage my heart. With some helpful direction from Richard Rohr I meditated on a Hebrew psalm. I slowly read the verse and then sat quietly listening. I read it again, each time making it shorter. It looked like this:

Be still and know that I am God.

Be still and know that I AM.

Be still and know.

Be still.

Be.[13]

For the first time in a long time I remembered that I was connected to God and His creation. By slowing and opening myself to God I was feeling what it meant to be alive. In this quiet space I was not defined by what I could produce. I mattered because I was known by I AM.

A life of programming combined with the expectations of my marriage had instilled in me a drive to produce, perform, achieve, and fix. There is little space to feel when you are always "on."

In a cabin in the Tennessee woods, in a little town in Israel, and in many places since, I have experienced what it means to Sabbath. I now long for moments of space and solitude. I have become an apprentice in the art of "unrehearsed living."[14]

   1. Stuck? Say it. Acknowledge it. Open your eyes.

   2. Stuck? Do something new. Find resistance and push through it.

   3. Stuck? Eliminate distractions. Create space and feel.

Chapter 4

THE NAMELESS WOMAN

You have made us for yourself, Lord, and our
hearts are restless until they rest in you.

Saint Augustine

A woman.
As a baby she wants to be held.
As a toddler she wants to be seen.
As a child she wants to be found.
As a teen she wants to be understood.
A woman wants to be loved.

When we get moving again and start pressing into the unknown, when we create space and have time to orient ourselves, we start to see what was previously in the dark. What we first uncover is usually not pretty: "Self … compliments you on rare occasions and criticizes you often."[1]

A boy and a girl both grew up in a bustling town by the sea. As time went by, they became well known for very different reasons. The girl in this story is nameless. The boy's name is Simon.

MASTERING RELIGION

Simon grew up in a comfortable middle-class home. His parents wanted him to become a scholar. He lived out their plan and studied hard. As a Pharisee, he became quite proficient in the understanding of his religion, which pivoted on six hundred daily rituals. Simon's religious mentors taught that God's approval was contingent on strict obedience to every command.

Simon excelled at following certain rules and skillfully faked it with others. It wasn't long before people identified him as a powerful leader. They admired his tenacity to hold high the ideals of the law. He became known as the expert, the man with all the answers. It was not uncommon for prominent, powerful citizens to visit his home.

But although he was intelligent, Simon was emotionally hollow and spiritually dry. Engulfed in his studies and consumed with the endless pressure to do everything right, he lost himself and any connection with the God he'd once known.

His heart was cold. A religious champion, and an emotional and spiritual weakling.

Man's sin is in his failure to live what he is. Being the master of the earth, man forgets that he is the servant of God.[2]

Abraham Joshua Heschel

In his failed attempt to perfectly keep these rules, Simon experienced rage, greed, sexual sin, and other moral breakdowns. The nature of his religion caused him to bear the weight of shame alone, hide it, and swiftly deflect and point out the failures of others. With his superior knowledge and religious formulas, Simon was a heavyweight contender. There were few who could spar with him.

One day a stranger came to town. The man began to teach in Simon's city with incredible insight. He spoke with an unusual confidence and authority. When he talked, Simon felt something. Memories of childhood. Moments of loving and being loved. Simon wasn't sure what to do with those emotions. His peers weren't sure what to do with this man.

Simon was intrigued.

He invited the man to his home for lunch. Lunch in those days in that particular city was a public spectacle. It took place in the home's centrally located open courtyard. People from all different social classes would come from around town to watch and listen to the diners pontificate and debate. One might describe this conversation as an ancient form of marketing and information exchange. Religious leaders and politicians could communicate many things to many people in a short period of time.

The teacher accepted the invitation to the meal.

Simon was pleased.

Simon knew that by having this radical in his home he risked offending his peers. It was nothing he couldn't navigate. *Hey, look, fellas. This guy is a phenom. I mean, if you watch the news, he's it. What better place to have him than underneath my surveillance? I'll watch him. I'll check him out. I'll find out who he really is.* Simon thought he had worked out all the angles. He was like a masterful attorney with a thorough knowledge of every law. *It shouldn't take much to identify Jesus' failure to keep them.*

In one of our meetings with Doyle, Angie produced a group of sticky notes that she had been collecting.

On them she had identified an exhaustive list of ways in which I was failing her as a husband. A catalog of grievances. Rules broken.

I remember vividly the weight of this judgment.

Sitting in the counseling office, I anticipated Doyle's response. Surely he would inform Angie that there was no way I was *that* awful. This would be a moment where he would come to my defense.

True to form, Doyle responded differently than I had hoped.

"That's not enough."

"What?" Angie replied.

"Jamie is messed up. He is way worse than that list describes. You need to add more."

Feeling the need to interject but not knowing what to say, I cautiously raised my hand like I was in a classroom.

Ignoring my gesture, Doyle continued, "The flesh is power-ful. The thoughts that go through our minds are laden with selfishness, lust, jealousy, greed. If you truly began to list off the sins any of us commits on any given day you would need more than just sticky notes. None of us could hold up to the scrutiny."

Jesus, on the other hand ...

HOPE

The girl grew up in the same town as Simon, but quite differently. Her family was poor. Her father worked several jobs and was rarely around. When he did show up, he was abusive. He left the family when she was very young, leaving an overwhelmed mother with too many children to care for on her own. The young girl learned to fend for herself. Sadly, horrifically, as a young woman, she figured out she could offer herself to men sexually and they would pay her in return. She learned to survive by turning this discovery into a business. Shame dominated her existence as day after day she prostituted herself in her hometown.

As time passed, her soul collapsed.

With her youth faded and her heart worn, she remained unsettled. Her loneliness was raw.

Each day was a battle—suppress the ache, keep moving, keep surviving.

Her business was successful.

She was good at her profession. She had quite a reputation.

Interestingly enough, the men who publicly scorned her privately admired her. It was a disgusting and twisted veneration.

One day, she saw the stranger. She watched as He performed a magical act on a man who'd had a shriveled, disfigured hand for as long as she had known him. What was once broken became whole. She was in awe. She'd never seen anything like it.

Later, on a walk through town, the woman overheard someone say the Healer was going to a hillside to teach. She followed the crowd at a distance. She couldn't help but notice that the man had a way with people; they were inexplicably drawn to Him. Jesus spoke words that were like a salve to her soul.

He performed more miracles and even challenged her religious tormentors through His teaching.

He talked about something called the kingdom and said to those sitting around Him,

> You know what? You are blessed.

> Even if you don't have a clue.

> Even if you have nothing.

> Even if you feel empty, as if your life is being snuffed out.

> You are blessed.

Why, you ask?

Because God is aware of you. He is a God who
loves well.

A blessing is the visible, perceptible,
effective proximity of God.

Dietrich Bonhoeffer

The woman listened to this man for over an hour and saw
gentleness in His posture. He finished teaching, and she
went back to town. For the next several days He was all
she could think about. She couldn't get Him out of her
mind. The images of masculine kindness were unlike anything she had ever imagined. He had awakened something
in her. Could it be?

She had forgotten what it felt like—but it was there.

She couldn't deny it.

Love.

She wondered what it would be like to feel accepted.

When she heard that the teacher had been invited to Simon
the Pharisee's house, she decided she would go. She moved
quickly. In her clothing, she tucked away an alabaster box.

AN UNINVITED GUEST

You can easily judge the character of others by how they treat those who can do nothing for them or to them.[3]

Malcolm Forbes

When the teacher arrived at the Pharisee's home, interestingly enough, Simon wasn't there to greet him. Earlier, Simon had calculated a plan and shared it with the other guests, made up mostly of Pharisees, religious scholars, and people of prominence.

"When this guy arrives, I've got to play this right," he told them. "I've heard that he is pretty good with words. Well, as you know, so am I! Gentlemen, I am setting up a verbal duel for your entertainment. Between the Romans and my own sect I know a great deal about the power of manipulation. We do this well—very well. Here's my plan: when he comes to the door, I'm not going to be there. A servant will let him in. Everything will be in place for my questioning and examination."

This scene unfolded by the Sea of Galilee, that same sea I had visited on my trip with the skeptic and the rock star. The climate is different from the southern Judean wilderness. The dirt is not dry and dusty; it is soft and rich, like topsoil. Depending on the weather, it can be very muddy. Not only was it cultural etiquette that a guest be welcomed with a handshake or a kiss, there would also be a basin of water to clean dirty feet and oil to refresh the guest's head. At Simon's house that day, the teacher received nothing.

Upon entering, the teacher was directed to the table, where the other guests were already positioned. The commoners crowded into the courtyard and huddled in the shadows, waiting to hear the conversation.

The stage was set.

Before lunch unfolded, however, the event was interrupted by a loud commotion. From out of the shadows a woman emerged. She lunged for the teacher. His humiliation, so reminiscent of her own, produced in her an unrestrained empathy, and the prostitute couldn't help but throw herself into the scene. With blatant disregard for Simon's agenda and common protocol, she kissed the teacher's feet. The commoners gasped and murmured about the embarrassing public display.

Then, silence. The chatty public ceased their conversations.

All eyes were on the whore who touched the one they called Jesus.

Tears spilled from her eyes.

She wept while leaning over Jesus' soiled feet.

She had no water or cloth to wash them.

Ignoring social decorum, she pulled her hair down and began to wipe each foot.

Her tears continued to fall. The filth and dirt slid off His skin.

The woman reached into her garment and from it revealed the alabaster box. From this box she pulled a flask of expensive perfume. She poured the fragrant oil over Jesus' feet, the aroma quickly overpowering the redolence of the meal. Her perfume, her primary form of advertisement and an ever-present reminder of her shame, was now gone. Compelled by a love she had never known until the present moment, she gave up the primary means of her occupation. An aroma once meant to allure now became an aroma of praise.

THE DIFFERENT FACES OF SHAME

Truth is, Simon and this woman were not all that different. They each had something to hide: shame.

Some of us train for years, like Simon, to find ways to bury our sin. Control becomes an effective means of shame management. We hold people at a distance and slowly, with limits and conditions, decide who is allowed in.

Legalists are not familiar with intimacy. They live with a false sense of security, one that is developed by judging other people and elevating themselves. A pharisee remains hyper-focused on behavior; this is how he keeps himself and others from exploring his heart. The more fault he can find in others, the easier it is to live in his delusional world.

Too often people are caught up in moralism, "constructing a way of life in which [they] have no need of a saving God.... Moralism works off of a base of human ability and arranges life in such a way that [their] good behavior will guarantee protection from punishment or disaster.... Moralism works from the outside: it imposes right behavior on oneself or others."[4]

Consider the frustration its proponents sit under.

All of life is constructed to fit some kind of external standard.

The immense internal tension is volatile.

If you are in this system, you can't maintain perfection, so your conscience eventually begins screaming about your inconsistency.

Soon you begin to hate yourself.

You feel like you are internally imploding. You feel like a sham, but you are in a system where you don't dare let anybody know. So you channel your self-loathing toward others. Pointing out their flaws, sitting in constant judgment regarding your fellow human beings, who keep overstepping your expectations of how you and the rest of the world should or should not be treated—"We use blame to deal with our feelings of powerlessness."[5]

Simon's self-talk began immediately after watching this intrusion in his home. He sat at the head of the table while judgment boiled inside of him. His thoughts are embedded in the story recorded by Luke in the Bible: "If this man were a prophet, he would know who is touching him and what kind of woman she is—that she is a sinner."[6]

It seems that Jesus knew Simon's thoughts. "Simon, I have something to tell you."

He began to tell a story: "There was a banker, a moneylender. He lent this man a day's wage, but he also lent another man the equivalent of an entire year's salary. The moneylender said to them, 'Hey, look, both of you. Your debts are forgiven.'"[7] (This would be a bit like your credit card company or the bank with your student loans calling and saying, "We have canceled your debt. We'll pay for the whole thing. Just ignore it. It's done.")

Jesus asked, "Now which of them will love [the moneylender] more?"[8]

"I suppose the one who had the bigger debt forgiven," Simon responded.

Jesus nodded. "You have judged correctly."[9]

The woman was still at Jesus' feet. The public was watching along with the other guests. There was a long pause. You could feel the tension in the air.

His eyes fixed on the woman, the teacher said to Simon,

> Do you see this woman? I came into your house. You did not give me any water for my feet, but she wet my feet with her tears and wiped them with her hair. You did not give me a kiss, but this woman, from the time I entered, has not stopped kissing my feet. You did not put oil on my head, but she has poured perfume on my feet. Therefore, I tell you, her many sins have been forgiven—as her great love has shown. But whoever has been forgiven little loves little.[10]

"There is a great irony here. If this woman had gone to Jesus' grave with this outpouring of affection and perfume, it would have been accepted, even admired. You were allowed to anoint a dead body, but it was not acceptable to express similar love and affection to a live one. Nothing has changed in two thousand years. We still save our best compliments and flowers for the funeral. Jesus' challenge here is for us to anoint each other while we are still alive."[11]

"Do you *see* this woman?" Jesus asked.

"Have you seen her as a little girl?

"Have you watched her through adolescence?

"Do you *see* in her the image of God?

"Do you *see* her?

"Because *I see her*. And I know her.

"You don't see her. You only cast judgment."

Jesus then looked at this woman and said, "Your faith has saved you. Shalom. Peace. Your shame is gone. It has been poured out. You are forgiven."[12]

This woman did not seek the approval of the elite.

She sought the affection of God.

What matters is not the quantity or depth of sin but the consciousness of it. Awareness.

To fully acknowledge one's shame is to give it to the one Person who smiles it away. He restores, forgives, and replaces shame with peace. If we are stuck, like Simon, and refuse to acknowledge or admit shame and brokenness, love will only leak from our souls.

> If you have been given mercy, you don't care who else gets it. Give it to the whole world for all you care, you are so thankful that you got it. But if you earned it, the opposite is true. If you earned it, you care. You care a lot. You care because you don't want anybody getting paid who hasn't worked as hard as you.[13]
>
> John Fischer

Some people experience so much self-condemnation that it screams from them. It shows up in the lines on their faces, their postures, their expressions, their impatience, their drive for control, their judgment. Their pain has little to do with all the people they have berated in the last seven days. Their hurt comes from their shame.

Lost in our own hurt, Angie and I could not really *see* each other.

I often felt the shame of failure. Angie often felt she could never measure up. I continued unsuccessfully rummaging for tools to fix our marriage and give Angie what she said she needed. Doyle introduced the term *over-functioning*. I had been over-functioning in my attempt to rescue Angie from her discontentment. A slice of my identity was connected to Angie's happiness.

While finding her way, Angie was still trying to get her bearings from whatever mood I was in. If I appeared tired, Angie assumed that meant I must be tired of her; if I seemed unhappy, that meant I was unhappy with her. Shame was triggered, and she felt rejected and unloved. Her dozens of books, synthesized into a rigid set of expectations, were meant to sustain her. These equations were supposed to work, but this man she was married to was a constant variable. Angie's alabaster box was her set of formulas. She was being confronted with the fear of finally breaking that box open and emptying it at Jesus' feet. My box was my fear of disapproval. I was slowly becoming aware of how great that fear really was.

> *Guilt and shame are both emotions of self-evaluation; however, that is where the similarities end. The majority of shame researchers agree that the difference between shame and guilt is best understood as the differences between "I am bad" (shame) and "I did something bad" (guilt). Shame is about who we are and guilt is about our behaviors.*[14]
> Brené Brown

Do you feel guilty about a particular struggle in your life?

Do you feel shame about that same struggle?

Guilt can be a motivator to change; shame paralyzes and keeps you stuck. "Exposure frees us to take in the humanity of our own failure and humiliation."[15]

LET IT GO

When you release your shame, you discover a love that is overwhelming. A love that dismantles your preoccupation with what others think about you.

This kind of faith triggers the power of God. Something changes within you. For the first time in a long time, you become acquainted with peace again. Peace is not the absence of problems or pain. It's the quiet confidence that you are not in control and that's perfectly fine. Peace exists when the shame dissipates and you begin to trust in someone other than yourself. On your best day you are not good enough for God. On your worst day you are not bad enough to run outside His reach.

Jesus wants you to experience love. Are you willing to let go of your alabaster box?

> The great and merciful surprise is that we come to
> God not by doing it right but by doing it wrong.[16]
>
> Richard Rohr

1. Stuck? Say it. Acknowledge it. Open your eyes.

2. Stuck? Do something new. Find resistance and push through it.

3. Stuck? Eliminate distractions. Create space and feel.

4. Stuck? Identify the obstacle. Speak out shame.

Chapter 5

STONE FENCES

There are only two ways to influence human behavior:
you can manipulate it or you can inspire it.... Manipulations
work ... [but] not a single one of them breeds loyalty.[1]

Simon Sinek

You train people how to treat you by how you treat yourself.

Martin Rutte

My seventh-grade teacher was the teacher from the comics. She wore the same patterned dress but in different colors. She had horn-rimmed glasses, and her gray hair was always up in a bun. Dandruff sprinkled down like snowflakes as she patrolled the aisles of her early adolescent subordinates.

And she was mean.

I can recall only a few smiles from her. She was a tough-as-nails woman who demanded order in her kingdom. One time a friend named Richie got in trouble for talking. She made him crawl under her desk and stay there.

Some time later, apparently forgetting that Richie was still there, our teacher sat down to grade some papers. The class, however, hadn't forgotten. They looked on in horror, wondering about their fellow classmate. After just a few seconds, Richie stuck his head out from beneath the front of the desk with a look of bewilderment. The class fell apart laughing. Our teacher, jumping up from her desk, yelled at Richie and then at us, letting us know that we would pay if there was not immediate order.

Sometimes mean people are funny people. Sometimes they are not.

HURTING PEOPLE HURT PEOPLE

In college, I did mission work in Brasil. I led a singing and drama team that performed in schools, orphanages, and theaters. We shared with people the love of God. I worked under a director who was often unkind. He intimidated many who worked for him. After each show, this man would find and berate me in front of my peers and the very people we were there to serve. He would tell me how incompetent I was, how what I did meant nothing to God or to the people I was talking to.

Twenty-two years later, I still remember one of our conversations vividly. With the benefit of the local missionary serving as my interpreter, I had just finished encouraging a crowd of several thousand people to find hope in God. I then prayed with them and walked offstage.

My director was waiting.

With a scowl and a firm grasp, he spun me around. He started the barrage, our noses close to touching. "Do you think those people were saved? Do you? They weren't saved! Those people are dying and going to hell, and you did nothing to help them!" He went on to explain that I had failed to use in my message key words from his salvation formula. (Remember our conversation about the "salvation prayer" in chapter 2?)

Tears streamed down my face.

They elicited no compassion.

This man had quite effectively shredded my spirit and my dignity. I was crushed. He seemed to find some sense of satisfaction in that. His associates waited until he was gone to find and try to encourage me. In management, I think this is referred to as "damage control." It was a kind attempt but did little to mend the wound.

In time I would learn that this type of leadership was not just my own experience. Chuck Swindoll writes:

> This legalistic style of strong-arm teaching is one of the most prevalent methods employed in evangelical circles. Grace is strangled in such a context. To make matters worse, those in authority are so intimidating, their authority is unquestioned.... The leader maintains strict control over the followers. Fellowship is based on whether there is full agreement. Herein lies the tragedy. This self-righteous, rigid standard becomes more important than relationships with individuals.[2]

I didn't understand it then, but hurting people hurt people. That is why they are mean. They didn't wake up one morning and turn on the mean switch. They are wounded, in need but refusing to acknowledge weakness. They are jealous of those who are happy. Free spirits, by the nature of their contrasted living, amplify the emptiness of resentful people.

It is an interesting thing, contrast. Without it we lack perspective.

In the fall, when you look up at the trees set against the sky, you see contrast. When the sky is blue, the autumn colors are illuminated. Blue causes you to appreciate orange, red causes you to appreciate blue, and so on. When the leaves are all the same color, their beauty is muted. Opposites, when placed next to each other, create contrast and often reveal perspective, even wonder.

When you love deeply, you hurt deeply. When you have felt the deep sting of rejection, you appreciate the gift of affirmation all the more.

Some of us live with the absence of mean people.

Some of us live with the absence of nice people.

Either way, our personal experience becomes our normal. Then one day we experience someone at the other extreme. We suddenly have a new perspective.

GIVERS AND TAKERS

Contrast becomes a teacher.

Have you ever tried to put two magnets together that have the same poles? What happens? Yes, they repel each other. One has to be turned around for them to connect. Sometimes the people we are most like are the people we don't connect with.

I have always heard, "Opposites attract. That's the way it's supposed to work in marriage. We fill in the gaps for each other." I suppose that is true, but I have wondered how universal *this* statement might be: Takers find givers; givers find takers. Doesn't this seem to happen often?

Based on their story, someone is used to receiving and taking.

And they do it well.

A blessing and a curse.

Based on their story, someone is used to giving and rescuing.

And they do it well.

A blessing and a curse.

Each person has trouble when the opposite is not around. It would seem the healthy person, the whole person, would have learned how to do both—both give and receive.

I have always admired the givers in my life and grew to have disdain for the takers. I watched and experienced what it was like to be abused by unrestrained and self-absorbed people. I didn't want to be like them.

What I failed to realize until now is that the martyrs in my life, those who took the abuse and lacked the willpower to fight or set healthy boundaries, were just as self-absorbed. They didn't want to feel pain. So they acquiesced. They deferred. They were terrible at receiving. Whether or not they wanted to admit it, martyrdom was often a control mechanism to keep them from becoming too vulnerable. They usually had trouble recognizing their own self-worth.

I did.

With a mixture of conscious desire to serve and subterranean motives to win approval, I rescued people. I wanted to keep them from pain. I knew the awful sting of being shamed. From my middle school years of being ridiculed through my college years of being shunned by spiritual authority and on into a marriage, I knew what it was like to feel rejected and unwanted. I wanted to help people avoid that awful ache.

I understood, at some level, that experiencing rejection was beneficial and shaped my story, but I sometimes had trouble watching others struggle and go through heartache. I especially had difficulty living in this tension with my wife. I was drowning and desperate for air.

It was becoming obvious to both Angie and me that I could no longer keep pace. We both needed to be exposed. We both needed to see our sin for what it was and then find freedom in the truth.

INVITATION ONLY

At one point our counselor looked at us and said, "Angie, you are the user, and Jamie, you are the dealer. Angie, your codependency[3] is an addiction. Jamie, you feed the addiction because you refuse to set boundaries. By attempting to be the ever-present deliverer for Angie, you are robbing her of the space she needs to find God. You have to let her struggle. Stop trying to fix everything."

I had failed Angie.

In my inability to set boundaries, I hadn't provided an environment for healthy communication.

We both went to work. It was not pretty. At times it was an emotional blood fest. Doyle warned us this much. He explained that we were both on separate surgical tables and that we would have to do the work without anesthesia. He said that it would feel really raw for a while. I had to learn to say, "No, I am not available," and Angie had to go through withdrawal. At one point I asked Doyle, "Are you sure I'm allowed to say that?!" I had been so duped by what had been modeled for me—by books, by Angie's expectations, even by elements of my Judeo-Christian heritage—that I couldn't fathom not being there whenever my wife needed me.

Doyle began to teach us the subtle difference between the words *need* and *desire*. For Angie and me, the phrase *I need you to do this for me* had become a control mechanism rooted in fear. It became a manipulative ploy to get what we wanted. Desire, on the other hand, was open-ended. It was invitational. It was like saying, "You may or may not be able to fulfill my wish, but I have enough inherent value to ask." The idea of requesting something that she might not receive was a massive paradigm shift for Angie.

Practicing a new language helped eliminate emotional triggers and forced us into a new way of relating. We began to say to each other, "I desire that you ..." While we were communicating a longing, it was up to the other person whether they could fulfill that desire.

There is a picture from my childhood that I think captures this concept. It is an image of Jesus standing at a door, knocking. He is a gentleman. He does not barge in. He does not coerce. He does not manipulate. He just says He has stopped by and desires to have dinner with me. It is up to me to invite Him in.

Angie tells the story that at one point she broke down with our counselor—"If I have to let go of all I am convinced marriage should be and start all over, this will never work! How do I know if Jamie will ever know or understand what I long for?"

Doyle replied, "Do you trust that God is big enough to tap him on the shoulder and let him know that you are in need?"

With tears, Angie said, "No ... no, I don't."

> *The world is rigged for frustration. There is a right way*
> *to do things, but we will never know for sure what that*
> *is. There is a way to make life work, but we will never*
> *do it right. No matter how we try, we will never be in*
> *control of our world.... [God] relentlessly undermines*
> *all that is not god to make room for ... God.*[4]
>
> Dan Allender and Tremper Longman III

My wife was still in the process of realizing the formulas she had fashioned that were supposed to produce sure outcomes weren't working. The scaffolding of her life was falling apart.

A militant radical once had an encounter with God and turned from the law to grace. He wrote this in a letter to a young church in the first century: "It is for freedom that Christ has set us free. Stand firm, then, and do not let yourselves be burdened again by a yoke of slavery."[5]

Angie was learning about grace.

I was learning about boundaries.

SETTING BOUNDARIES

A healthy boundary is like a fence that outlines your identity. As Henry Cloud and John Townsend explain, "Boundaries are anything that helps to differentiate you from someone else, or shows where you begin and end.... Boundaries help us to define what is *not* on our property and what we are *not* responsible for."[6]

"If I do not 'own' my life," they continue pointedly, "my choices and options become very limited."[7]

My initial homework from Doyle was to check in with my heart and see how much emotional energy I had to give. If I had none, I was to tell Angie that. I was also to gently remind her that what was going on with me had nothing to do with her. My energy or lack of it did not define her. I simply did not have what she needed in that moment. Angie's homework was to stop managing, stand down, and give space for God's Spirit to move.

This was no easy task. A codependent who doesn't get feedback is like a crack addict who's not getting crack. The compulsion of the addict is to do whatever is necessary to feed the addiction. The early days, weeks, and months were not easy. Angie subconsciously would attempt to outmaneuver my boundaries. And sometimes I would get the boundary thing all wrong. Have you ever played Chutes and Ladders? Imagine it never ending. This is often how we both felt.

On one occasion Angie started raising her voice. I told her she wasn't going to talk to me that way. My response to her anger didn't go over too well, nor was it effective. I went in to see Doyle a few days later and said, "This whole boundary gig is not working. I tried it and had zero control over what Angie was doing."

Doyle patiently explained to me that my response to Angie wasn't setting boundaries. What I had done was attempt to limit her. One cannot limit or control the other person. He or she has the freedom of choice. What I could do, however, was set limits on myself.

This was what my new boundary-setting language sounded like: "Honey, if you choose to raise your voice, I am going to remove myself from this conversation." This was difficult for Angie, but she was beginning to understand value decisions. For instance, she began asking herself which had more value in the moment: raising her voice in frustration or having meaningful emotional connection later. She began to grasp that setting boundaries had more to do with me than with her.

Had I had these tools as a student missionary in Brasil, my response to my spiritual authority might have sounded like this: "Sir, you are my spiritual director, and you speak often of the image of God. I bear that image. I would not serve you well to allow you to continue in your verbal violence toward me. You are my authority. When you regain self-control, regardless of whether or not I agree, I am willing to listen to your opinion and observation. In the meantime, I remove myself from this conversation." Whether he respected me for my self-care or kicked me off the team was irrelevant. That would be his choice. I would have protected my heart, and in the long run, that would always be more important than standing on a stage.

ICE

My friend Bob uses this term for setting boundaries for kids: ICE.[8]

Instruction. Identify your expectations.

Consequence. Communicate the responsibility expected and the consequence if it's ignored.

Experience. Give them space to exercise their options.

For example, at the time of this writing, seven-year-old Addie was at the dinner table one night and didn't want to eat her food. It was six o'clock, and she said she was tired. I said, "Well, you have two options: (I) We expect you to eat your food. (C) However, you can go to bed two and a half hours early, right now if you like, and not eat. (E) Exercise your options.

She attempted negotiations. I stopped her and repeated myself: "Those are your choices. You are free to choose."

She ate her food.

Incidentally, the next night Addie and I went out on a daddy-daughter date. We were driving when she asked me, "Do you want to buy me some ice cream?"

I told her, "Well, you already had a treat today, so I'm not sure."

"Would you like to give me a kiss?"

"Yes, I'd love to."

Addie paused. "Exercise your options."

"Okay, I'll take the kiss." I smiled.

Addie looked at me in the rearview mirror, a bit puzzled, then realized she hadn't set me up quite right. I laughed, and she smiled. "How did you do that with me yesterday? What are the words again?"

She is a smart cookie.

Setting boundaries takes practice. It can be challenging. You will go through trial and error. But don't give up just because you get it wrong a few times.

Be very cautious of people who attempt to shame you for failing. You might share my tendency to give everyone but yourself the benefit of the doubt. You trust everyone else's motives first and yours last. This openness and loving spirit can be a wonderful thing, but when you and I fail to love ourselves well, we have trouble loving our "neighbor" the way we should.

You have to cut yourself some slack too. When you get it wrong, own it. Apologize if needed. Then go back to the drawing board.

THE POWER OF NO

If you are like me, there is one word that is harder to say above all others.

No.

And no is "the most basic boundary setting word."[9]

For those of us who prefer pleasing people, *no* feels conclusive and abrupt. And for those of us who have experienced people in our lives who ignored the word when it was employed, deep down we wonder if we even have the moral imperative to use it. We incessantly question our motives, thinking maybe we are doing something wrong. Takers exploit this. They come hard and fast and take from us before we even know something is gone.

When you have to interact with other people, especially those with strong personalities, do you experience this?

Trying harder doesn't work.

Being nice out of fear doesn't work.

Taking responsibility for those people doesn't work.[10]

How many of us have lived months, maybe even years, staring at the nail in front of us and using the above ways of relating like a saw, a screwdriver, and a tape measure, all to no avail? Why? Because we failed to use the most basic of tools: the hammer. In other words—no. Simple. To the point. No maneuvering or twisting. No qualifying. Just hits the nail on the head: no.

Years ago I did mission work in Ireland. I was struck by the country's landscape and beauty. As is often displayed in pictures, the land is replete with meandering stone fences that go on for miles.

I asked an Irishman about them. He told me that in many cases those fences mark off the boundary lines of someone's land. He also said that when the land was first farmed, the stones were a great nuisance to farmers. Soon, however, the farmers realized that they needed those stones to build fences. The wind could be quite fierce. Without those stone fences, their land would erode and no longer produce sustenance.

Have you felt like you were eroding inside?

The force of others' expectations slowly wearing you down?

They are all around you.

Stones that seemed like obstacles.

Failures and experiences that seemed too numerous to consider.

But not now.

You are waking up.

Risking again.

You have taken your hand off the plow long enough to survey the landscape of your life.

There are some tools nearby that you have neglected. Use them

Say no when it is not your responsibility.

Say, "I am not available for you right now," when you don't have the emotional energy.

Stop giving out of compulsion or duty.

Stop blaming someone else for the way you feel.

Stop rescuing people and stealing the problems they need to own.

Stop living in fear.

It is time to redeem those failures.

Learn from them.

Use them now for your own good.

Go, and build fences!

> *1. Stuck? Say it. Acknowledge it. Open your eyes.*

> *2. Stuck? Do something new. Find resistance and push through it.*

> *3. Stuck? Eliminate distractions. Create space and feel.*

> *4. Stuck? Identify the obstacle. Speak out shame.*

> *5. Stuck? Set boundaries. Learn to say no.*

Chapter 6

THE GIFT OF SUFFERING

*Inside every block of stone or marble dwells a
beautiful statue; one need only to remove the excess
material to reveal the work of art within.*

Michelangelo

*What we obtain too cheap, we esteem too lightly —
'Tis dearness only that gives every thing its value.*

Thomas Paine, December 19, 1776

I am not really into pain.

I don't schedule it on my iCal.

I don't look forward to it or pray for it.

When I am in it, I usually ask God to get me out of it.

But I cannot deny that I learn more through pain than I do through comfort. Suffering produces more in me than success does.

I wish I could be the exception to the rule.

I wish I were not like the rest of the human race.

But alas, I am a descendant of Adam and carry the brokenness and default of my splintered design.

SOUL ACHE

While the journey for Angie and me into interdependence was needed and ultimately freeing for both of us, the process was unbelievably painful. We discovered that breaking old ways of relating took courage and a willingness to exist with a soul ache. There was much we didn't get right.

We got bite-sized morsels of wisdom from our counselor, but it seemed we were often left choking. More than once, Angie or I rushed off to Doyle's office, asking for an emotional Heimlich maneuver. And more than once he had to help us spit out what we couldn't digest ... only to make us swallow it again.

On one occasion while visiting Angie's family in Alabama, we decided to leave our kids with their grandparents and go out on a date.

Before long the conversation went south.

Only this time, something strange and unusual occurred.

I didn't care at all about what Angie was saying. I was pleasantly unaffected. More than that, I was somewhat amused.

I didn't feel anxious or angry.

I felt like I had left the restaurant to dwell on a remote planet equipped with some telescopic device that allowed me to look in on the conversation from afar. Of course, this aloofness caused Angie's codependency to escalate. Not only was I not giving her identifiable signals to interpret, I was giving her nothing at all. Truthfully, the whole experience felt euphoric. I had done it! This was what implementing boundaries was all about!

Angle was going nuclear, and I turned into a stoner.

As you might imagine, my euphoria didn't last. Everything unraveled. Angie's anger peaked, but her harsh words and raised voice still were unable to evoke feedback from me. We walked out of the restaurant, parrying barbs about divorce. Things were such a disaster that we packed up and left the next morning without speaking to each other the entire trip home.

We went to see Doyle the next day, separately. I told him what had happened and how brilliant he was and what a good student I had become.

"You *still suck* at boundaries." Doyle has a unique way of getting to the point.

"What?!" I asked incredulously.

"You did not effectively set boundaries; you simply disassociated."

Oh, boy, a new term.

"What does that mean?"

"It means Jamie has left the building. It means you were not present. You did not stay in the tension, do the work, feel through your pain. You checked out."

"But it felt so good."

"Sure it did—temporarily you avoided feeling hurt. Your flesh can manufacture all kinds of ways to self-destruct. You didn't behave in any way that would provoke understanding and healing. You simply deferred pain."

Years ago I read a book by Neil Postman called *Amusing Ourselves to Death.* The premise of the book is that many of us in Western culture are obsessed with amusement and leisure. I think this obsession is a way of keeping ourselves distracted from our real pain. If we don't have to see it, we can pretend it isn't there.

But it is.

THE HIDDEN DEEP

When I think about how to handle pain, I see myself as a kid in a pool, trying to hold a plastic ball underwater. Eventually the ball slips from my hands and comes flying out of the water. And more than once, it smacks me in the face.

What you submerge eventually finds its way to the surface.

The deeper it is submerged, the greater the splash.

For some people, it becomes natural to keep that ball underwater at whatever cost. Sometimes without even realizing it.

I have met people who seem shallow. They have trouble moving the conversation past weather, food, or football. When you drop down to the deeper things about life, they look at you glassy-eyed as if you're speaking Icelandic.

They truly have no idea what you are talking about.

For a while this frustrated me in my interactions with people.

In time I have come to have compassion for them.

They hurt someone or were hurt. Deeply.

And so they disassociate. They live a life of pretend.

In *The Exquisite Risk*, Mark Nepo writes,

> We tend to occupy ourselves with worrisome activities and preoccupations in order to divert ourselves from the necessary task of feeling what is ours alone to feel. Rather than feel our loneliness, we will run nakedly to strangers. Rather than feel the brunt of being abandoned, we will construct excuse after excuse to reframe the relationship. Rather than feel our sadness and disappointment, we will replay the event to ourselves and others like a film with no ending. It is this cultivation of neurosis and all its scripts that feeds the drama of our bleeding.[1]

How many of us slept around in college to deal with the pain of loneliness?

How many of us were abandoned by our father and spent a lifetime making excuses for him?

How many of us have failed miserably at something, and rather than own it and grow from it we keep talking about how we didn't get a break and someone else did and how unfair it was?

You know what? We just keep bleeding. We can't even begin to heal the wound, because we pretend the wound isn't there. This abused and overused but apropos *Monty Python* quote could not be more relevant:

> King Arthur: [after Arthur's cut off both of the Black Knight's arms] Look, you stupid [expletive]. You've got no arms left.
>
> Black Knight: Yes I have.
>
> King Arthur: *Look!*
>
> Black Knight: It's just a flesh wound.[2]

This satire is such a display of the denial we often live in.

We are wounded.

Suffering.

Our arms and legs have been cut off. We are unable to give or receive, but we refuse to acknowledge it.

> *Deep in every human soul is a deep desire to justify yourself....*
> *We're afraid that we're not okay, that we're not desirable.*[3]
>
> Tim Keller

Angie says that the great pain underneath her quest for control was ultimately her fear of being unlovable. She managed everything she could to try to keep that fear in its cage. Understanding our value is so central to all of life.

For some time I didn't value myself enough to recognize my own suffering. I had learned to accept and expect pain as part of life. But accepting it is not the same as feeling it. I was good at parking pain off to the side. It seems that is a coping mechanism, the disassociation that Doyle spoke of. We fail to understand that eventually the ball is going to come shooting out of the water. It is just a matter of when and how.

THE GREAT TEACHER

My friend Don, a teacher and coach, was born with a hole in his heart. He was unaware of the condition.

As the years passed, blood gathered around his lungs.

The blood began to rot. When he was forty-seven years old, the decaying blood caused a massive stroke, and he was left paralyzed on the left side of his body.

Don's family was shocked. He was a young and physically fit man. None of it made sense.

The doctors operated and during surgery discovered the defect in his heart. If his body hadn't suffered the stroke, his heart would have eventually just shut down.

His suffering revealed a hole that desperately needed attention.

"Illness is the doctor to whom we pay most heed: to kindness, to knowledge we make promises only; pain we obey."[4] If we will listen, pain is and will always be a teacher.

This became very clear to me as I listened to a World War II bomber pilot, a personal friend, speak to a group of teenagers. He made a powerful and dramatic statement: "I hope you will never have to see the things I have seen."

I have studied a bit of culture and history. I was always confounded with how the Greatest Generation, as Tom Brokaw famously named them, gave birth to the notoriously selfish baby boomer generation.

As I listened to this veteran, it dawned on me. In his generation's sincere attempts to prevent their children from experiencing pain, those children grew up entitled. The Greatest Generation was great precisely because they had suffered so deeply.

I read recently about some older Londoners who were interviewed about their lives. Upon reflection, they stated that the most precious times of their lives were in the early 1940s, when they were constantly being bombed by Germany. While they wanted the war to end, while they wanted and even needed to be out of harm's way, it was in the trials and difficulties that they truly lived.

Few of us welcome trials, but it is undeniable that, like contrast, suffering is a great instructor.

We learn through struggle and difficulty.

One Sunday after I gave a message about struggle, my friend Karen gave me a children's book she had written called *Far Flutterby*. It tells the story of a caterpillar stuck in a cocoon.

In her wonderful way, Karen reminded the reader that it is in the struggle that we get unstuck.

In the struggle we break free.

In the struggle we find our wings.

One night, when my struggle in our marriage was at its heaviest and I was feeling the weight of everything bearing down on me, I sat on the floor, opened my Bible, and asked God to show me something.

I had been reading in the book of John, and I came across a passage where Jesus was teaching. He said, "Very truly I tell you, unless a kernel of wheat falls to the ground and dies, it remains only a single seed. But if it dies, it produces many seeds."[6]

I wrote in the margin, "So, God ... You are killing me."

It felt that way.

And looking back, He was.

God was killing off my ego and self-confidence.

I would have to admit I could not keep going on my own.

I was learning to trust Him in deeper ways than I had ever imagined.

Death reminds us that something is fundamentally flawed.

Something about life is not working according to its design.

We feel this at a soul level.

We are forced to grieve and acknowledge that there must have been an ancient plan for things to play out differently.

I think we each grapple with a persistent question: is this it? I think the Ancient Way whispers back: no, this is not the end.

GET HONEST

Mark Nepo writes about a woman who

> kept hiding her sadness in books, reading about other lives, as a way to deny the pain of her own story. This kept her undeveloped. Eventually she was in her quiet room, her small fire burning, another novel on her lap, and she couldn't read another word, because her eyes just wouldn't stop watering. She couldn't see the words, because her own untold river was overflowing the dam of her silence. It wasn't tears, she would later say, but the water of her life finally rising into her days. Against her will, her need to form inwardly wouldn't go away.[7]

And neither will yours.

You were hurt.

You were abused, manipulated, abandoned.

It mattered.

It did.

It mattered.

But it is time to enter that pain.

Stop pretending the awful gash isn't there.

Acknowledge the pain that flows like blood from an open wound.

I understand it is easier to watch sitcoms and get lost in reality TV shows. I get that. But you will never fully heal until you get alone with God. Quiet your soul. Listen. Cry out

And don't think this is just an event you can put on the calendar. It is a process. We must die to ourselves daily.

Some of you would just rather have a formula—a specific Bible verse to claim, a mantra to chant, a law to follow. As if that will cause you to heal and grow. But: "The only people who grow in truth are those who are humble and honest.... Without these two qualities we don't grow..... Humility and honesty are really the same thing..... A humble person is simply a person who is brutally honest about the whole truth.... [Most] growth in the spiritual life (and this is surprising to capitalists) takes place not by acquisition of something new.... It is accomplished by the release of our current defense postures, by the letting go of fear.... Thus we grow by subtraction much more than by addition."[8]

YOU ARE NOT ALONE

Think about this: suffering is universal.

No one escapes it. The question is and will always be, What *form* will your particular suffering take?

Jesus said that each one of us must bear our own cross.

Paul the apostle spoke of a thorn in his side.

Each one of us will suffer.

"Your pain is the concrete way in which you participate in the pain of humanity."[9] When we realize we all suffer, we see reflected back the other forms of pain worn by our brothers and sisters who live and have lived on this same rock. Our pain connects with their pain, and when our eyes are opened to this, we experience validation.

We are not crazy.

We are not alone.

And not just humankind, but all of creation cries out for mercy.

Along with hope, the realization of universal suffering should produce humility.

If you have not yet loved or suffered enough to clear out your narcissism, then you will not naturally promote other people's uniqueness and value. If you wonder why you have trouble connecting with others, this is probably why.

People intuit in conversation with you when you deflect or self-promote. They may not be able to put their finger on it, but people will eventually drift away, knowing that there is a barricade to connection.

In some cases they will come up with reasons to avoid you because your disconnection reflects theirs.

Not long ago I had breakfast with a friend. When I first moved to town, I asked him to join me in a new enterprise. Reluctant at first, he eventually jumped in. He and his family were instrumental in serving and helping make this vision a reality.

We were in it together for many years.

Even before he asked me to breakfast, I already knew what he was going to say. He was moving on.

Funny how you can feel the energy between you and someone else change without knowing why or how.

"We're leaving," he said, getting right to the point while sipping his coffee.

"I know," I replied.

He talked about how he and his family didn't feel connected anymore.

It was time to try someplace new.

I asked him if I had permission to speak freely.

He kindly invited me to do so. I said, "Bro, I think there is more to this story, and I believe it has to do with your soul. You are either carrying shame you are afraid to uncover or a wound you are afraid to tend."

He replied, "Well, I should have guessed that you would not have just politely said good-bye and let that be the end of it." Thanking me, he acknowledged that he knew he had a pattern of shutting people out, never getting too close to anyone. He just didn't know why. We ended the conversation with a hug and a good-bye. He is a good man, and my love for him remains deep. Whether or not he ever chooses to fully live is up to him.

God would like to show you the land of deep relationship.

However, like the discovery of any new territory, finding this land takes time.

Like a savory meal. Good food is never fast. There is a journey involved. Preparation. Experimentation. A variety of ingredients that come together to create abundant flavor and nutrition. Relationships happen the same way. They are not instantaneous.

There is hope for you. On the other side of suffering, a kingdom filled with love and meaningful connection waits to be discovered. The choice is yours: Will you choose to do more than exist? Can you find the courage to face your past, explore your story, and prevent the rotten blood from compressing your heart? You do not have to go alone. A fellowship awaits. There is strength in numbers. Keep moving—the healing will continue as you fight off isolation and open yourself to others.

1. Stuck? Say it. Acknowledge it. Open your eyes.

2. Stuck? Do something new. Find resistance and push through it.

3. Stuck? Eliminate distractions. Create space and feel.

4. Stuck? Identify the obstacle. Speak out shame.

5. Stuck? Set boundaries. Learn to say no.

6. Stuck? Recognize the value of suffering. Feel through your pain.

Chapter 7

TELL ME A STORY

The universe is made of stories, not of atoms.[1]

Muriel Rukeyser

As a rough rule of thumb, if you belong to no
groups but decide to join one, you cut your
risk of dying over the next year in half.[2]

Professor Robert Putnam

Back in 2005, after we had moved to Tennessee and shortly
after we started our church, I sensed God calling me out of
the house as if we were meant to have a very significant
conversation.

I heard this whisper in my heart: *Go to the woods, and listen*
for Me.

Whenever I hear something like that, I always wonder if I am making it up, if it's the remnants of the previous night's dinner or if it's truly the voice of God. But since faith is entering the unknown, I got into my car, drove off, and looked for a place to walk into the woods. Not having lived in Franklin, Tennessee, long, I didn't know exactly where I was going. I turned down Split Log Road, as that sounded promising.

A few minutes later, I pulled over to the side of the road. Sure enough, there was a leaf-strewn path leading into the woods. It was November 2, a beautiful fall day. I found a place to stand and looked up into the sky.

TOUCH SOMEONE'S LIFE

My conversation with God went like this:

"I know You wanted to meet with me today. Sounds like You have something in mind. But before You get rolling, do You mind if I say something?"

Sure.

"Thank You. One basic, overarching question. Why did You send me to plant a church in Franklin, Tennessee? It seems like there is a church on every corner. I mean, people introduce themselves here and ask, 'What church do you go to?' This is crazy. Why didn't You send me to Brasil? Seriously, why am I here?"

Are you finished?

"Uh. Yeah."

Wrong question.

"Huh?"

You need to get over yourself.

This is My story, not yours.

I will send you where I wish.

Jamie, all of your life you have told people you want to 'change the world for God.' And at times, your motives were pure. But all too often, you wanted to change the world for Jamie.

I know your story.

No friends in middle school, a misfit in college, an underdog mentality from an underdog town.

Let's be honest, much of your life has been about proving your worth.

"Oww. Okay. Yeah.

"Can't deny it.

"I am sorry.

"I repent."

Rather than change the world, I want you to touch the life of someone else who will change the world.

This statement would alter my life forever. I stared for a while at this point—at the trees, the sky, the leaves. There was something solemn about the moment.

Touch the life of someone else who will change the world.

Do you understand what I am saying?

"Yes, I think so. I'm supposed to empower other people and let them get the credit. As much as I love 'the stage,' I am supposed to lean into subtlety and move away from the 'big show.' Rather than a bold and brash, clean and shiny church, we are supposed to become a quiet but confident family of faith. Rather than wave the banner and give the cheer, we will invite the broken and steadily serve whomever we find in need. And along the way, You will use someone other than me to influence the world."

You have the idea.

"God, I have spent most of my life trying to become a great leader, and very little of it learning to become a *great listener*. Starting today, I'll begin seeing people not as chess pieces to move around in a grand strategy, but rather as stories that are unique and magnificent, individuals to be released to their God-designed life."

I left the woods, wondering if I was crazy. Was this a dream? Was I just good at monologuing? While I didn't hear an audible voice, it was as if there was an echo in my soul. And there was one something I couldn't deny: I felt deeply loved. And so, that day, my mustard-seed-sized faith chose to believe that the Creator of the world invited me for a walk in the woods and gave me a reason to sing.

LISTEN TO UNDERSTAND

Life leaks out of us as we find ourselves treated as objects, roles, images, economic potential, commodities, consumers.[3]

Eugene Peterson

I talked earlier how in the dawning of our young church, Angie and I began to see human beings as true image bearers of God.

People were no longer assets or converts or numbers to count.

Each person became more deeply than ever before an individual story, a person created, shaped, designed, and adored by God.

Angie and I had to make this application with each other.

Could we see each other as more than a husband or wife and all the expectations that came with those titles?

Would we be willing to slow everything down—cease the word sparring—and really listen to each other? I am stirred by this statement: "To listen is to continually give up all expectation and to give our attention, completely and freshly, to what is before us.... To listen is to lean in, softly, with a willingness to be changed by what we hear."[4]

Thus a new journey began. Rather than waiting to speak, Angie and I began listening to understand. This is a very different form of communication. Previously we just waited for the other person to take a breath. Then we jumped in with our contrasting opinion or harsh analysis. It was an exchange of commentary, not a conversation.

I think this happens not just in marriages but in all relationships. Think about it.

When is the last time you were with someone who listened to understand? When was the last time *you* listened to understand?

How often do you have conversations where it is obvious the other person could not care less about what you are saying? They're just being polite enough to let you finish before they tell their story or describe in endless detail their recent accomplishments.

How many people do you know who truly listen? Some of us long to be known, yet no one has taken the time to listen to the chorus of our lives, let alone the verses.

And so we go on living a hollow existence—and "if the story of your soul is *never* told, if the secrets of your heart are *never* shared, if the struggles in your life are *never* heard, then you are living the tragedy of an unobserved life."[5]

My grandfather never spoke much. He lived a life of pain. It seemed like in his mind he was always somewhere else. He died in 1979. All we had to interpret his story was an old newspaper clipping and what he had left behind in a cigar box full of trinkets. I remember wishing he had left a journal, a diary, or something revealing. While going through his stuff, my father, my grandmother, and I read the article he had saved. It told the story of a truck driver whose brakes went out. The truck lost control, and as it was careening off a hill the driver leaped from the vehicle and survived with only minor injuries.

The driver was identified as Bob George. I was a kid at the time, and as my grandmother finished reading I exclaimed, "That's Grandpa!" She looked at the date and thought back— "You know, I remember Bob coming home with an injured shoulder one night. He never did tell me how it happened."

Without his story we were left with only a junk drawer to determine what had meaning in his life.

So many people are afraid to share the details of their pasts.

It seems better to leave things hidden. Unsaid. I suppose this would be true if relationships didn't matter.

A STORY WORTH TELLING

The only way we will know one another is to know one another's stories.

It is in this knowing that we will learn to love well.

In 2006, the movie *Rocky Balboa* was released, sixteen years after the last sequel. My sons were around eleven at the time, and I had them watch the first four movies on DVD. (We didn't watch the fifth, as it should never have been made.)

We got a sitter for the girls, and Angie and I and the boys watched the return of Rocky on the big screen. In the middle of the film, not necessarily at a highly emotionally charged moment, Angie looked over at me and asked, "Are you crying?" At which point the boys leaned over and looked to see why Mom was prompted to ask such a question. Sure enough, they saw a tear rolling down my cheek.

Angie continued, this time in a softer voice, "What's wrong with you?"

I leaned toward her, not taking my eyes off the screen. "I've missed him."

"Who?" Angie whispered.

"Rocky."

"You've missed Rocky?" Angie looked confused.

"Yes."

"But he isn't real."

"I know."

"You're weird."

After the movie I explained. "I don't know why I was so emotional. I guess it kind of felt like I was hanging out with a favorite uncle that I hadn't seen in a long time. I mean, think about it, Ang. We have been through a lot together."

"Who? You and me?"

"No, me and Rocky!"

Angie rolled her eyes and laughed.

"Hey, listen, I ran with him through the streets of Philly. I was ringside when he beat Apollo. I sat next to him when Mick died—that was terrible. I rode with him in his Lamborghini while 'No Easy Way Out' was playing and he was trying to find himself. I was with him in his failures and in his triumphs. And tonight we were reunited!"

Why did I feel so connected to a guy who isn't even real?

I knew his story.

Every one of us has a story worth being told. It doesn't matter if your story feels plain and uninteresting. It doesn't matter if you think your story will make someone's hair stand on end. No one else on the planet is exactly like you. No one else has your story.

God has uniquely crafted you. Even the discarded debris of your life.

The stuff you have brought on yourself and the junk that has been thrust upon you.

The betrayal, the mistakes, the abandonment, the loss—in God's economy it can all be recycled, reclaimed, and used for good.

I came across a book recently that discussed new discoveries in neuroscience. Recent research concluded that "an important part of how people change—not just their experiences, but also their brains—is through the process of telling their stories to an empathic listener. When a person tells her story and is truly heard and understood, both she and the listener undergo actual changes in their brain circuitry. They feel a greater sense of emotional and relational connection, decreased anxiety, and greater awareness of and compassion for others' suffering."[6]

Because Angie's hurt usually expressed itself in anger, I was endlessly defensive. I had trouble empathizing because I didn't recognize Angie's sadness. When I looked past the anger to her story, I began to see Angie with new eyes. I began to see her as I was learning to see others. Angie was the child who wanted to be found, and the teen who wanted to be understood, and the woman who longed to be loved.

Her story, its pain and its triumphs, were woven into His story.

SOUL ENVIRONMENT

Every story represents a unique person with a specific role to play.

In order for a story to be gifted—to tell your story is a gift—there must be a listener. Good ones are hard to find. To listen empathetically, to receive without judgment, and to really care about the person and what's being said is an act of love. When someone vulnerably shares his or her story and someone else empathetically listens, energy is exchanged.

Sadly, churches often fail at this. I hear all the time about people who share their stories and shortly thereafter are shunned. I think the reason for this is the mirroring effect a story has upon a listener. If you are asleep, you don't want someone reflecting back the shame that you have buried. Because somewhere along the way, many church people thought they were supposed to reflect perfection, they cover up their sin and shame. They wear plastic smiles while they welcome you and furrowed brows when they suggest you aren't the right fit.

There is no group of people that models empathetic listening and vulnerability better than Alcoholics Anonymous.

The fifth of the famed twelve steps says that one is "admitting to God, to ourselves, and to another human being the exact nature of our wrongs." The very first pastor wrote this to guide the then fledgling movement called Christianity: "Confess your sins to each other and pray for each other so that you may be healed."[7] This urban pastor and many addicts under-stand something fundamental to life. Telling our story is like cleaning out the compost of our soul.

Since that day on Split Log Road, we have attempted to build our church around this premise.

Each of us, deep down, longs to be known. When we are able to tell our story, the achievements and the struggles, to an empathetic listener, something changes inside us. The ancients used to call this *katharsis*. When we empty ourselves of our shame, it is like "the removing of clouds so the sun can shine through."[8]

In our church we have groups of people who get together intentionally to hang out, care for one another, and engage in spiritual conversation. We call these groups "villages." A village is a safe place where we can share failures and progress. I started a village of just guys with Mark, the musician I introduced in chapter 1. We invited well-traveled men who were experienced enough to know that accomplishments meant little in life without relationships. Mark's bandmate Will had a farm, and before long a village began to form around a weekly campfire behind his barn.

There I experienced firsthand the power of speaking out my frustration with my own sin and brokenness.

By sharing my struggles and questions I realized something:

I was not alone.

When I kept it all inside,
     my bones turned to powder,
     my words became daylong groans.

The pressure never let up;
     all the juices of my life dried up.

Then I let it all out;
     I said, "I'll make a clean breast of my
          failures to GOD."

Suddenly the pressure was gone—
     my guilt dissolved,
     my sin disappeared.[9]

                    A Hebrew psalm

This village filled a tank that was easily emptied in other places. It was crazy how the process worked. Someone would say something, often a piece of his own story, and I would find validation, perspective, answers, and—perhaps most significantly—hope.

Angie had pressed into a village of her own. She met a handful of women while going through a seminar led by friends of ours. They bonded and afterward continued to meet. Angie discovered that women enjoy processing more than most men and that some of what I could not give her could be found in deep and meaningful relationships with other women. Angie and these women have diverse backgrounds and varying personalities, but they carry a trust birthed in their vulnerable exchange of stories.

There is no such thing as instant community.

A relationship is an experience built on moments of relating.

The greater the accumulation and flavor of these moments, the deeper the relationship.

The more honest and genuine those moments, the healthier the relationship.

The starting place for a soul environment is the fertile ground of storytelling.

IN THE PRESENCE OF TRUTH

I have discovered something through the years.

Few people have ever told their story in narrative form.

It takes patience to listen to someone tell their story. Most meander through unnecessary details while trying to recall the pieces that fit to describe the whole. As a listener, you learn that's okay. Telling your story is like looking around in a junk drawer (or a cigar box) and evaluating what's worth telling, what has value.

To help people, I often ask, "Tell me about the moments that changed the direction of your life."

This gives people signposts that help them recount their journey.

If you will listen with your soul to theirs, you will hear something.

This may take some practice, but if you do this long enough, you will discover what I have heard countless times.

The echo of eternity.

You have to pay attention because most people, while describing their lives, only drop down into their hearts for brief moments. But when someone chooses to be vulnerable, his or her honesty reveals truth. And "what's fascinating about truth is that we know when we are in its presence."[10]

Every time I listen to a story—*every time*—I hear redemption. Why?

Because I am convinced that there is an Author and that He is good. I have seen this promise fulfilled repeatedly: "He has made everything beautiful *in its time*."[11]

Once we spend time in someone's story, we see them differently. Judgments fade as we identify with the universal struggle that our stories reflect. Their look, their dress, their race, their accent—all these things disappear when we see their soul. Empathy is drawn up from the well of our being. We see the imprint of God. We love well.

The journey that follows is an exciting exploration for how to "spur one another on toward love and good deeds."[12] We no longer see someone as a resource for making our lives better, our business benefited, or our church bigger—but rather we humbly watch and pray and challenge and encourage our friend as they leap from the cliff and break free from the cocoon.

A NEW WAY TO LOVE

Guided by Doyle and inspired by the stories of others, Angie and I began risking for love. At first it was awkward and uncomfortable, but we pressed on. I was learning to process out loud, to share how I was feeling while I was feeling it. This is not always easy, and to this day sometimes I don't know what I am feeling until a few days later. One night while out to dinner, I shared with Angie that I felt sad. She asked why. I explained that as a pastor, I went home from work every day knowing that I left people disappointed. I knew that there were those who wanted a quicker reply to an email, or needed to get my counsel on some life decision but were unable to do so, or could have used a thank-you note or word of encouragement—and that's not including the folks who just wanted to hang out. I told Angie I didn't know why this affected me so much, but it did. I just knew that on one hand I deeply cared for people, and on the other I was afraid of someone feeling unwanted, as I had for so many years.

As a shepherd, something to grieve.

As an approval seeker, something to release.

She listened and pondered my story.

That night, something happened in her. The way she tells it, she began to see me in a detached way. No longer just as a husband or resource that existed to meet her needs—she began to see me as a person, a friend. The internal work she was doing was paying off. Seeds sown were growing into flowers preparing to bloom. Angie was learning to give and not just take. She was waking up! My vulnerability met her empathy and found a mooring. And a new way of loving was finding its way in both of us.

Brené Brown poignantly sums up the significance of the dance between vulnerability and listening:

> Vulnerability is neither comfortable nor excruciating, but necessary.
>
> What makes us vulnerable is what makes us beautiful.
>
> We are wired for struggle, but we are worthy of love and belonging.
>
> We must let ourselves be seen. Deeply seen.[13]

It is not as hard as you might think.

Maybe even start with a mom or dad or grandparent or neighbor or pastor or priest.

Smiling, try something like this: "Hey, Mom—tell me your story."

1. *Stuck? Say it. Acknowledge it. Open your eyes*

2. *Stuck? Do something new. Find resistance and push through it.*

3. *Stuck? Eliminate distractions. Create space and feel.*

4. *Stuck? Identify the obstacle. Speak out shame.*

5. *Stuck? Set boundaries. Learn to say no.*

6. Stuck? Recognize the value of suffering. Feel through your pain.

7. Stuck? Listen to someone else's story. Be vulnerable with yours.

Chapter 8

LIFE IS A SETUP

The art of being wise is the art of knowing what to overlook.[1]
William James

When your greatest heartache becomes your
greatest ministry, grace has come full circle.
Bethany P. Haley

A boy named Jacob grows up in a home where favoritism is the order of the day. His mother obsesses over him; his father favors his twin brother. Jacob continues the pattern as an adult.

Jacob marries twice. He is tricked into marrying Leah, his first wife. His second, Leah's sister, Rachel, is his favorite and everyone knows it. The family dynamics are chaotic. Jacob has a total of twelve children with both wives and even the family housemaids. It becomes obvious quickly that his favorite child is Joseph, the firstborn son of Rachel.

Jacob uses Joseph as an emotional surrogate to feed his codependency. Seventeen-year-old Joseph acts out the script set before him. He is arrogant and self-indulgent.

God seems to have a way of using the people one would least expect.

God speaks to Joseph in a dream and offers him a preview of his destiny.

While sleeping, Joseph watches a short film of his future. In it his brothers bow down to him.

Joseph wakes up. What a movie.

The way he sees it, he is the star.

Joseph wastes little time in sharing the vision with his brothers. And he does it in dramatic fashion.

SOLD FOR SILVER

Joseph's father had given him—and no one else—an expensive, ornamented tunic. He walks up to his brothers, wearing this coat, which is essentially a billboard announcing, "The favorite son has arrived." He tells his brothers the cheerful news: "God has showed me in a dream that you will all bow down to me!"

This does not go over well.

Joseph's relationship with his brothers is already character-ized by envy and jealousy. Most of them are older, married, and have kids.

They don't like Joseph.

He isn't invited to babysit his nieces and nephews because he's a punk.

To be fair, the brothers have their own issues.

Their lives have been characterized by patterns of deceit, betrayal, violence, and greed. They have little patience for an obnoxious, self-absorbed teenage brother who is grand-standing about his future rule.

One day while the older brothers are grazing their flocks, away from Joseph, a scheme is introduced on how to shut up Daddy's favorite once and for all. The following quote is from the biblical narrative in Genesis 37:

> Come now, let's kill him and throw him into one of these cisterns and say that a ferocious animal devoured him.[2]

An intense conversation ensues, and the oldest, Reuben, steps up (he often tries to be the hero): "I'm not sure we should actually kill Joseph. Just saying, that feels a little over the top."[3]

Judah speaks up. He's got a better plan.

"Hey! Let's sell him!"[4]

With a family like this, who needs enemies?

The brothers settle on throwing Joseph into an empty cistern and fabricating his death to their father with a story about him being killed by a wild beast. In reality, they eventually sell him off to a nomadic group of merchants for twenty pieces of silver. Their annoying brother is gone forever. Or so they think.

This is a pretty intense act of betrayal.

Joseph has been sold up the river (well, actually, the desert).

He will never return home.

A MAN OF CHARACTER

As we have already determined, suffering has a way of waking us up to truth. Struggle reveals what we previously couldn't see. But that still does not justify the evil done to us, just as it does not justify the evil we do to others.

It hurts to be ignored, rejected, and betrayed. We often reject the salve of forgiveness because we misunderstand its medicinal properties. As a result, many of us live with a bitterly infected wound.

Joseph is taken to Egypt and sold to Potiphar, a member of the political elite who works directly for Pharaoh, the king. Potiphar is in a significant position of influence—maybe even the captain of the guard, the head of the secret service, according to some historians. He is a powerful, well-respected man. Joseph works for Potiphar for eleven years.

> *Pain is inevitable, but misery is optional.*[5]
> Tim Hansel

Joseph does not disintegrate into a heap of self-pity. Quite the opposite.

As his world gets bigger, it becomes clear to him that he is not at the center. His attitude changes, and as time passes he presses deeply into his faith in God. Phrases like "and God was with Joseph" and "Joseph trusted God" are repeated throughout Joseph's story.

It seems the blessing that pours out over Joseph's life is directly connected to this truth: "God is trustworthy."

With his mother's good looks, his great-grandfather's legacy of faith, and the blessing of God, Joseph makes an impression. In time, he earns Potiphar's trust and becomes the administrator of his entire estate.

Trust is a fragile thing. For a man, there are a few things, like a flattering woman, that will test his loyalty.

Potiphar trusts Joseph; that is crucial to the young man's success. Joseph knows it. He never intends to be anything but trustworthy.

But Potiphar's wife takes an interest in the new man of the house. She attempts to lure Joseph into her bed by slowly chipping away at his boundaries.

"Joseph! Come here. Come see me."

He is hesitant. Resistant. But week after week, she flashes her eyes and bares her shoulders.

Perhaps the most difficult to resist is the temptation that is patient.

It begins with small compromises, setting you up for the big one.

Eventually, this temptress shows her cards, so to speak.

"Joseph, come to bed with me."[6]

He is close enough to smell her perfume, to feel her breath. Her hand slides up his arm, and the alarm bells go off like an air-raid drill. Joseph turns and sprints out of the room. But not before she reaches for him and grasps his tunic.

In that time in Africa, a man wore a tunic and nothing else.

The executive director is streaking through the estate.

Has Potiphar's wife got a story! And she is filled with rage because she didn't get what she wanted.

With a vile tongue, she spews lies to her husband, betraying Joseph's hard-earned trust:

"That slave that you brought into this house tried to rape me!"

Potiphar acts on his wife's accusations and throws Joseph into a dungeon.[7]

Once again, Joseph has been betrayed.

Once again, he has been stripped of his clothes.

Once again, he is back in a pit.

And once again, rather than descend into victimization and self-pity, Joseph remains strong. He organizes his small domain, and the warden takes notice. Leadership has a way of rising to the top. Joseph is given the task of administrating the entire penitentiary. His character cannot be ignored.

> *Character doesn't rise to the occasion, but*
> *is revealed by the occasion.*[8]
> Colonel Jeff O'Leary

A handful of winters go by, and two influential men who worked closely with Pharaoh are thrown into jail with Joseph. One was Pharaoh's baker, the other his cupbearer. The cupbearer had an interesting job. Not only was he the guy who guarded the king's food and drink against poison by tasting it first, he also functioned in an executive capacity. He managed Pharaoh's schedule and determined who would or would not get an audience with the king.

The mighty have fallen. They are downtrodden and forlorn. Gloomy.

Joseph walks up to them. "What's up, fellas? I run the place. Can I interest you in a corner cell?"

They ignore his sarcasm and blurt out, "We each had these dreams, and it is killing us not knowing what they mean."[9]

At that time Egypt actually offered dream-interpreting schools called Houses of Light.

Joseph didn't go to school for this, but he has a special gift. A gift he has had since he was a teen. They tell him their dreams, and he explains them.

Joseph says to the baker,

"You're going to die. Soon.

"Your head is going to be cut off. Your body is going to be impaled on a pole. And the Egyptian police are going to hang your body parts on display for everyone to see.

"I guess any hope for a reality show is out of the question. Sorry."[10]

The baker is aghast. "But, but ..."

Joseph puts a finger over his lips and points to the baker's buddy. "Shhh. It's his turn."

Joseph says to the cupbearer,

"You are going to be reinstated. The charges are going to be dropped. You're going to be back in your former role of leadership.

"Now, when you go back to Pharaoh I'm only asking for one thing—don't forget me, okay?

"Look at me. Focus. Remember me. I am not supposed to be here."[11]

The cupbearer enthusiastically responds, "Oh, yeah, yeah, yeah. Sure!"

But he doesn't. He completely forgets about Joseph.[12]

If there was ever a man who should have abandonment issues, Joseph is the guy. But he doesn't. Instead he leans into God, the only one who has stood by him and loved him well.

STRUGGLE'S NEW NAME: OPPORTUNITY

Two years go by. Pharaoh has a dream.

The dream team—and I mean a literal dream team—rolls up and takes on the challenge.

But they are stumped.

Pharaoh is frustrated. Nobody gets it.

"No, no, no, you guys are not interpreting this dream correctly.
I would know."

The cupbearer has a lucid moment. He tells Pharaoh about
Joseph.

Pharaoh says, "Bring him to me."

In that culture, which was pretty unique in the ancient world,
everyone was clean-shaven. The king's attendants hustle to
make Joseph presentable and bring him to the king.

Pharaoh says, "Here's my dream."

Joseph listens and responds with confidence, "Easy. Here's
the interpretation: Egypt and her surrounding nations are
going to experience seven years of incredible abundance.
It's going to be amazing, more than anyone's ever seen.
Following those seven years, there will be a famine unlike
anyone has ever seen. Life will feel like a Tim Burton film.
Colors will fade, and people will get really, really skinny."[13]

Joseph pauses to allow the information to sink in. Then, not
one to miss an opportune moment, he boldly follows up with
a recommendation: "Might be a good idea to tax the people
for the first seven years, take a portion of what they have.

Remember, everyone will have an abundance anyway, and much will be wasted, as people will be unaware or disbelieving of what will happen in the future. People will live as if they'll always have more than enough. If you listen to what I'm saying and plan and store for the famine, you'll be able to care for everyone in need."

Joseph presses further: "I think it's a good idea to find a man of wisdom who is skilled with administrative and executive gifts to run this campaign."[14]

Carpe diem.

Looking at his attendants, Pharaoh says, "Well, nobody else has figured out my dream. This guy totally nailed it, and he's got a great plan. Who's wiser than this guy?"

Then, turning to Joseph: "I want you to do it."[15]

Pharaoh gives him his ring and officially makes him second in charge of the world's reigning superpower. In a sudden turn of events, Joseph, the assistant to the warden in Precinct 39, the dungeon on the far edge of the territory, becomes the viceroy, the executive just beneath the king.

We have much to learn from Joseph.

Anyone can learn from any experience.

Every struggle creates an opportunity for growth.

It doesn't matter if you've gotten the shaft. It doesn't matter if you were abandoned. It doesn't matter if you were betrayed, abused, or falsely accused.

It would have been easy for Joseph to pull the victim card. Over and over and over again, he is the victim.

He could have sat sulking in jail.

"I didn't do anything wrong!"

"This is unbelievable!"

"I resisted temptation I was a man of integrity. And what did it get me?"

"God, where were You?"

"Why did You abandon me?"

What would your attitude have been?

> *Consider it pure joy, my brothers and sisters, whenever*
> *you face trials of many kinds, because you know*
> *that the testing of your faith produces perseverance.*

Let perseverance finish its work so that you may be
mature and complete, not lacking anything.[16]

James, the brother of Jesus

Joseph does not choose victimization. He says, "I can learn anywhere, and you know what? I'm going to keep developing my skills. Need help leading? Sure, I'll organize the jail. I learned how to motivate and empower servants. Now I will learn how to do the same with a bunch of thugs."

Talk about perspective.

Malcolm Gladwell made the fascinating observation that those who have true expertise in something have acquired their extraordinary abilities, among other factors, through a minimum of ten thousand hours of practice. Between his time in Potiphar's house and his time in the prison, Joseph spent thirteen years administrating—more than enough time to accumulate ten thousand hours. When it's time to play the role God designed for him, Joseph does so with unimaginable success.

Joseph's story is not over.

It's worth pausing to consider:

What is your current attitude regarding your feelings of rejection and abandonment?

What is the current disposition of your heart?

Are you feeling victimized by your spouse's unfaithfulness?

Are you allowing your father's neglect to take root in your heart?

Are you living under the shadow of a past betrayal?

PATTERN RECOGNITION

Angie and I had to fight through feelings of victimization. Either we could focus on how we felt mistreated by people in our stories and by each other, or we could ask how God was using what we were learning to give attention to His redemptive work in the world. We didn't know it at the time, but God was equipping us with new relational tools forged in the furnace of suffering, to nurture the garden of relationships sowed around us.

One day Angie and I were sitting on the couch at home and started discussing the idea of sharing our inadequacies in front of our church family. In our past church experiences, lots of speakers shared stories of triumphs and successes, but only a few shared how they were working through their mess.

So we did. Angie had never spoken in front of a group that size and had tremendous courage to be so publicly honest. We both admitted our failures and dysfunctions and even introduced the church to Doyle, thanking him for his navigation. We closed our talk by asking if there were other couples who struggled in their marriages. As you might imagine, we were not alone. There was a sweet sense of unity as men and women in similar circumstances joined us around the stage and asked for prayer.

My friend Mike is a captain in the Marine Corps. He says that doctrine, education, and training mean nothing without "operational experience." A significant part of operational experience is pattern recognition. This is the ability to recognize what has happened in the past while at the same time anticipating what's ahead. Mike is not saying that one becomes a clairvoyant armed with precision accuracy regarding the future, but rather that with pattern recognition one gains greater understanding of the present.

As Angie and I emerged on the other side of our pain and started to gain traction with our new tools, we began to see clearer. We were able to identify patterns not only in ourselves but in our home. We have twin boys. They have shared a room, often been mistaken for each other, have had the same mentors and coaches, and by and large have had the same environment that has shaped their lives. And yet in the midst of all this sameness, the central features of their personalities are nothing alike.

Jordan we call, "Fire. Aim. Reconsider."

Tyler we call, "Ready. Ready. Ready. Aim. Consider firing."

Jordan has had several girlfriends.

Tyler is waiting for the right one.

For some time, Jordan had great difficulty breathing. He had seen many doctors and specialists, and we were frustrated because none offered a concrete diagnosis. Eventually he had exploratory surgery. Yet again, doctors told us that Jordan looked healthy and they could not find anything conclusive that explained his distress. Still, the symptoms were getting progressively worse. One day we met with a good friend, Dr. Chris Motley, who has a unique approach to medicine. He asked Jordan some questions and sensed that our son's trouble was of an emotional nature. Chris asked if anyone in our family had a problem with boundary setting. Angie looked at me, and I looked out the door and down the hall. She pointed her bouncing finger at me and smiled.

I grimaced. "Uhh, yeah, so that would be me."

In the days and weeks that followed, Angie and I began to unpack with our children what we were learning about ourselves and what we could see in them.

Jordan began recognizing patterns.

If someone was in need, he was immediately available.

His empathy, a great gift, was becoming a powerful weakness. Jordan was so willing to give his heart away and to own people's struggles that he became physically, emotionally, and spiritually depleted. He had trouble saying no. He had difficulty saying he wasn't available. Eventually, Jordan was able to identify his deficiency in boundary setting. He is learning to lean deeply into his faith and is finding strength and healing.

Tyler had trouble entrusting his heart to others. He taught himself to carefully read people and in time started becoming what he thought others wanted him to be. Angie was able to share with him what she was learning. She talked about how special he was as God's unique creation and how important it was for him to not focus so much on doing the right thing but on becoming the right person. Less concerned with how people view him, Tyler is working on giving his energy to being fully present and enjoying relationships around him.

God was already redeeming Angie's and my failures with each other by equipping our children with emotional tools that they otherwise might never have received.

What if all of life is a setup?

The rejection. The betrayal. The abandonment. The suffering. The pain.

What if you are being equipped now for what you will need later on?

Isn't this the story of every great adventure?

When we live with our hands open, we remain open and ready to receive.

We become learners, students of life.

Take inventory. How have you been equipped?

What have your struggles taught you?

How have they prepared you for something bigger?

How has your life been a setup?

Is it possible that God has allowed the cistern of your soul to empty only to be refilled with the pure, living water of genuine love?

Though the circumstances were not ideal, Joseph's life was rich with experience. He was being trained and didn't know it. Without the humiliation and suffering, the slavery and imprisonment, he could never have acquired the skills and relationships he would later need and have. And for Joseph, the adventure had only just begun.

God's words are rarely a spotlight down the path. But He promises they will be a lamp unto your feet.[17]

My sons were invited to try out for a television reality show where judges evaluate your musical ability. After a day of painful waiting, they auditioned in front of four celebrity judges and thousands of people in the Charleston Coliseum. They had never sung in front of a group larger than one hundred and twenty people, and here they were as teens attempting to impress the judges enough to go to the next round. Their nerves took over, their voices wavered, and with one yes and three noes they were sent home. When they returned to Nashville they shared the news with friends who had been pulling for them. Alan, one of our musician friends, pulled the boys aside and said, "Look, I believe in motion. I want to help you keep things moving." Within thirty days, Alan and his team put the boys in the studio, recorded a four-song EP, filmed a video, and launched a YouTube channel.

Their three noes turned into a four-song EP and an incredible online response to their music (TheGeorgeTwins.com).

Don't be discouraged when you suffer setbacks, when you feel locked up, when it seems no one remembers you. You are being prepared for something. Believe that.

Keep moving. You're doing great!

Who knows? Maybe the next dream to be fulfilled is yours.

1. Stuck? Say it. Acknowledge it. Open your eyes.

2. Stuck? Do something new. Find resistance and push through it.

3. Stuck? Eliminate distractions. Create space and feel.

4. Stuck? Identify the obstacle. Speak out shame.

5. Stuck? Set boundaries. Learn to say no.

6. Stuck? Recognize the value of suffering. Feel through your pain.

7. Stuck? Listen to someone else's story. Be vulnerable with yours.

8. Stuck? Take inventory. List what you have learned.

Chapter 9

REUNION

*Given the right combination of circumstances, we are all
capable of unspeakable deeds. When we turn perpetrators
into monsters, we deny this common ground between us.*[1]

Paula Huston

*We often forge the bonds of our lives from
the scraps of ones that were broken.*

We pick up Joseph's story in a pristine palace where the
onetime prisoner is loving life. Seven years of abundance. So
much abundance, in fact, that after years of record keeping,
Joseph and his accounting team just stop counting.

Life is good. Joseph gets married. He has two boys, Manasseh and Ephraim. Manasseh means "to forget." Ephraim means "doubly fruitful."[2]

It's as if Joseph said,

> There is much that was taken from me; however I
> have been given a new life.

> God is pouring out an abundance of blessing, and
> I am moving on.

However, true to life, just about the time you're unstuck, feeling good, cruising ...

Here comes the past.

The old life suddenly arrives in a Winnebago.

The famine strikes. Neighboring countries are completely unprepared.

Back in Joseph's hometown in Israel, his father learns that there is grain in Egypt. He looks at his sons and asks, "Why do you just keep looking at each other? ... Go down there and buy some for us, so that we may live and not die."[3] So Jacob sends them, with the exception of the youngest, Benjamin, to get food.

Jacob's favoritism has shifted from Joseph to Benjamin, his only child left from Rachel, his favorite wife. His parenting skills have not improved. If Jacob were in therapy, he would learn a great deal about the term *enmeshment*.[4]

To be fair, his decision is not without good reason. The last time he trusted his other sons with one of Rachel's kids, the boy's coat of many colors came back with blood on it. Jacob does not want to lose another son, so he keeps Benjamin close to his side.

Once they arrive in Egypt, the brothers gain an audience before the viceroy, who is responsible for distributing the grain to foreigners. They bow in honor to the leader of the land and plead their case. What they don't know is that they are kneeling before the very brother they betrayed into slavery.

Joseph is stunned. Like the hyena attacked by Richard Parker,[5] he is assaulted by a memory he had hidden a long time ago. There, in front of his very eyes are his brothers ...

And they are bowing before him

His dream has come true.

Have you ever had a dream come true? Sometimes a scene you pictured in your mind becomes reality, but the scenes that got you there were more unbelievable than you could have imagined.

I'll bet it was like that for Joseph.

It was like that for Angie and me.

Recently in a worship gathering with our church, Angie and I walked toward the Communion table together. Our children met us in line. We took Communion and bowed to pray together. Addie was in the back with our children's ministry, but Ashton was with us and lovingly displayed compassion as she prayed for a friend. Ashton is a kindhearted young woman who welcomes everyone she meets with the same unbiased enthusiasm. Our sons, deeply moved by God that morning, poured out their hearts. Standing there in a circle with our family, surrounded by close to a thousand people, Angie and I began to cry. When it came to planting a new church, ripping open our marriage was not in our plans—but somehow God used us, and a church was birthed in the midst of our brokenness. Somehow our children were captured by the divine romance, and here we stood, looking into each other's eyes, experiencing a dream come true.

REOPENED WOUNDS

Unexpectedly, Joseph is placed in the difficult and awkward situation of having to interact with his betrayers.

His heart is flooded with conflicting emotions.

His two worlds collide.

His brothers don't recognize Joseph, so he leaves his identity concealed and begins a charade.

Though he knows Hebrew, he speaks to them in Egyptian and uses an interpreter to translate into their native tongue:

"You are spies."

"No, my lord," they answer. "Your servants have come to buy food. We are all the sons of one man. Your servants are honest men, not spies."[6]

Because Joseph followed God, he must have had a desire within him for things to be right with his family. Doyle often reminded Angie and me, "The Spirit is a reconciliatory Spirit."

The nature of God is to restore and reestablish connection. This doesn't mean, however, that you willingly enter into a conniving, abusive relationship again. What have we learned? Healthy relationships come with boundaries.

If we want to help someone recognize the way they hurt us—rather than just shove the offense down their throat—we might tell them a story or use a metaphor to help bring about awareness and offer perspective. Joseph wants to know if his brothers have changed, and he displays compassion in the process. Rather than just tell them a story, Joseph, because of his position of power, tests them by dramatically re-creating a narrative:

> If you are honest men, let one of your brothers stay here in prison, while the rest of you go and take grain back for your starving households. But you must bring your youngest brother to me, so that your words may be verified and that you may not die.[7]

They instantly feel fear and remember their disgrace and betrayal. Like a ball shooting out of the water, their shame is immediately before them.

> Surely we are being punished because of our brother. We saw how distressed he was when he pleaded with us for his life, but we would not listen; that's why this distress has come on us.[8]

These guys had been carrying around this shame all these years.

Listening in on their Hebrew dialogue, Joseph is overwhelmed by emotion. The narrative from the book of Genesis is laden with sadness: "He turned away from them and began to weep."[9]

What do you do when you thought you had moved past hurt, bitterness, anxiety ... and something rips open the wound?

You may be moving forward. Growing up, gaining ground, loving well.

That is real. Don't discount the truth that you are maturing and changing.

But sometimes we haven't gotten to the root of our pain. Most of us don't voluntarily dig down to the depths that are needed. Digging up old stuff stinks. It may be rotten, but it's not dead yet.

And like a cold-case file, when you open it up years later, your forensic instincts are usually better. With time you gain new perspective.

Joseph could have chosen revenge in response. Revenge can give us a feeling of power. Most action movies are designed this way. We spend about an hour and a half working up a thorough hatred of the villain, so that when the hero shoots him in the kneecaps or stabs him violently in the neck we cheer and rejoice in the justice that has been dispensed. I suppose there are some films that deal with this sense of justice in redemptive ways, but most just play to our appetite for revenge. It is hard to forgive when we are betrayed.

Joseph realizes he has an opportunity. His past has been thrust upon him, but he doesn't resist or run. He does something else instead.

AN ONGOING TEST

Joseph emotionally gathers himself and reengages his brothers. Simeon is seized as collateral.

Joseph gives the brothers grain in exchange for their silver and then tells them to go. Silver plays a crucial role in this story. Remember how much he was sold for when his brothers jettisoned him as a teen?

Joseph tells his lead steward, "Stick their money back in their pack and send them on their way." The steward does as he is told. The experiment is in motion.[10]

On the way home, the brothers find the silver. It has come back to haunt them. They fill their father in on what has happened in the palace and how they are supposed to return with Benjamin to prove that they aren't spies. Jacob refuses. Simeon sits in jail.[11]

Time goes by, and eventually they run out of food again.

Jacob and his sons have a meeting at the family conference table. Reuben speaks first: "Dad, we've got to go back to

Egypt. I'll go and take Benjamin with me. If I don't come back with your precious son safe and sound, you can kill both my sons!" Jacob wonders how he could have produced such foolish offspring and stares at Reuben, dumbfounded: "You're an idiot. I've already lost Joseph. And if I lose Benjamin, I'm supposed to kill your sons? Oh, that's a bright plan, Reuben."[12]

Taking leadership, Judah pipes up and says, "Here's the thing, Dad—I get the whole deal with not wanting Benjamin to die, but we will all be dead in a couple of weeks 'cause we're out of food unless we go back. Let me carry the responsibility, and I will bear the blame if I don't return with your son."

Jacob finally relents. "All right, fine, go—but just so you know, I am heartbroken! I can't believe you're taking my Benjamin."[13]

> So the men took the gifts and double the amount
> of silver, and Benjamin also.... When Joseph saw
> Benjamin with them, he said to the steward of his
> house, "Take these men to my house ... they are to
> eat with me at noon." ... Now the men were fright-
> ened when they were taken to his house. They
> thought, "We were brought here because of the
> silver that was put back into our sacks the first time.
> He wants to attack us and overpower us and seize
> us as slaves and take our donkeys."[14]

The brothers are a bit irrational—"He wants to attack us and overpower us and seize us as slaves and take our donkeys."

Fear, shame, and guilt—together they will make you think you're going to lose your ass.

Joseph's steward assures the brothers that all is well. He provides for their needs and returns Simeon to them.

They present Joseph with gifts, and he asks, "How is your aged father you told me about? Is he still living?"[15]

They reply, "Your servant our father is still alive and well."[16] And they bow down, prostrating themselves before him.

Dream fulfilled.

And there, among his betrayers, his loyal little brother grown into a young man.

Emotion begins to spin like a tornado in Joseph.

> Deeply moved at the sight of his brother, Joseph hurried out and looked for a place to weep. He went to his private room and wept there.[17]

Joseph can't hold it together. All the boys back together again.

And he is the only one who knows.

Joseph lives from the heart. He is fully present and not afraid of emotion.

The test he proctors for his brothers is clearly painful and difficult. He tries to pretend that he is harsh, angry, and authoritarian, but his heart keeps taking over. Joseph's sensitivity and compassion are two of the hallmarks of his leadership. He lives as an open soul. And that soul is being challenged once again.

Joseph returns to the meal. And continues the ruse.

"Serve the food."

The brothers eat, they drink (too much), and their trepidation is erased. Dinner and cocktails with the vice president, their brother released from prison—life is good![18]

The next day, the brothers get ready to leave. Food has been resupplied—and the payment is again sneaked back into their sacks. The silver keeps coming back to haunt them.

This time, however, more than just the money is planted in their travel gear. A large chalice called a divining goblet is hidden in Benjamin's satchel. (The goblet was probably a gift from the House of Light Dream Center in honor of how Joseph saved the nation through his wisdom and dream-interpretation skills. Fanciful speculation on my part, but a distinct possibility.)[19]

MOMENT OF TRUTH

The drama continues. Joseph's steward catches the brothers as they leave the city and accuses them of stealing. The men are searched, and the goblet is found in Benjamin's hipster messenger bag. There is no other option. Benjamin must be taken into slavery.[20]

This, of course, is the moment of truth. The concerto Joseph has been composing builds to its crescendo.

The score, the movie, the novel,

the turn,

the tide goes out and the world holds its breath.

How will Joseph's brothers respond *this* time? Will these ten Hebrew men keep their blood money and leave another brother in slavery? Are these the same cruel men who had betrayed Joseph, or have the reminders of their evil ways produced brokenness? They don't know it, but their response bears the weight of a nation. Joseph sits at home with his leg hanging over one side of a chair, staring off into space. All he can do now is wait.

The brothers rip their clothes, an outward sign of grief, and return to Joseph's house. Regardless of whose fault it is, regardless of how the blame might be weighed and balanced, one brother, Judah, continues his journey out of the shadows. Listen to him take responsibility. In bold are the words to give extra attention.

> Joseph was still in his house when Judah and his brothers came in, and they threw themselves to the ground before him. Joseph said to them, "What is this you have done? Don't you know that a man like me can find out things by divination?"
>
> "What can we say to my lord?" Judah replied. "What can we say? How can we prove our innocence? **God** has uncovered [our] guilt. **We** are now [your] slaves—**we** ourselves and the one who was found to have the cup."[21]

Judah is saying, "Though the guilt lies with our brother, we will all stand beside him and share the punishment." The brothers were guilty of stealing Joseph from his father, their anger stoked by Joseph's claim that he could see into the future.

But this time the brothers are innocent of the crime of stealing from Joseph. And when he tells them he can see into the future, they are not angry but repentant. What a setup! Joseph masterfully re-creates the entire scene of his betrayal with his little brother as his stand-in and a goblet to symbolize his dream!

Joseph offers his brothers an opportunity to come face-to-face with their guilt, to see it for what it really is, to acknowledge it, to repent of it, to turn from their wicked ways, and to ultimately find salvation.

Judah asks for permission to step closer. He explains that Benjamin is the only son left from his father's favorite wife. He tells Joseph that if Benjamin does not return, he is quite sure his father will give up living.[22]

Judah is passionately truthful, perhaps for the first time in his life.

He doesn't know that he confesses his sin to the one he has sinned against.

Read this last part of the narrative slowly and feel the emotion in this exchange.

> Now then, please let [me] remain here as my lord's slave in place of the boy, and let the boy return with his brothers. How can I go back to my father if the boy is not with me? No! Do not let me see the misery that would come on my father.[23]

The one who conceived the plan to sell Joseph now offers himself as a substitute for his father's current favorite.

Years later, one of his descendants would offer Himself as a substitute for you and me.

Joseph can no longer control himself, and he releases the emotions that he has held captive. He speaks to his attendants:

> "Have everyone leave my presence!" So there
> was no one with Joseph when he made himself
> known to his brothers. He wept so loudly that the
> Egyptians heard him, and Pharaoh's household
> heard about it.[24]

Tho interpreter is gone, and Joseph speaks in his native tongue.

"It's me.

"I ...

"am ...

"Joseph."[25]

> But his brothers were not able to answer him
> because they were terrified at his presence. Then
> Joseph said to his brothers, "Come close to me."[26]

Joseph lifts his arms in the air and motions with his hands in the gesture of an embrace. He is bridging the physical distance and the emotional distance in the same moment. The brothers move in closer to Joseph, so close that the years fade away and the features of Joseph's face start to become familiar again. Joseph clasps one hand around Benjamin's neck and the other on Judah's shoulder.

"I am your brother Joseph."

Reconciliation is about more than just forgiving. It's about reconnecting. It's about peace … shalom.

A CHANGE OF HEART

I wish I could have experienced certain moments in history.

Sitting in a chair near a Pennsylvania farmhouse and listening to our sixteenth president give his address while looking over a battlefield.

Standing on the deck of the USS *Arkansas* and watching the fate of nations hang in the balance while young men from around the world run onto a beach in France, courageously exchanging their lives for freedom.

Listening to an African-American preacher in Atlanta stand up to violence, using the power of passionate words of truth.

Sitting on the side of a mountain by the sea, listening to Jesus teach, tell stories, and make me laugh.

I also wish I could have been in North Africa, standing near a circle of twelve Hebrew men who had just experienced a plot twist they could have never imagined.

> I am your brother Joseph, the one you sold into Egypt! And now, do not be distressed and do not be angry with yourselves.[27]

Joseph is centered. He is both confident and compassionate.

Don't blame this on yourselves. Don't be angry at yourselves for selling me here, because it was to save lives that I suffered!

It was to save lives that God sent me ahead of you.

It was to save your lives.

Joseph tells them to get their father and their families and relocate them to Egypt. He will make sure the entire clan is cared for.

> He threw his arms around his brother Benjamin and wept, and Benjamin embraced him, weeping. And he kissed all his brothers and wept over them. Afterward his brothers talked with him.[28]

This is not a story of rejection. It is a story of reconciliation.

This is not a story of condemnation. It is a story of redemption.

This is not a story of revenge. It is a story of forgiveness.

You don't get to satisfy your guilt by repaying the silver.

No, it comes only through a change of heart, a different disposition, a transformation. Joseph knows this. And this is precisely why he carries his brothers through the crucible of shame and guilt to help get them to the other side.

THE POWER TO CHOOSE

Forgiveness is not a relinquishment of boundaries.

Forgiveness does not mean someone gets to abuse you.

Forgiveness is about you more than it is about them. Forgiveness is about letting go so that nothing festers inside your heart. Forgiveness exists for your physical, emotional, and spiritual vitality.

The weak can never forgive. Forgiveness
is an attribute of the strong.

Gandhi

Was Joseph the victim? Yes. Did his own family unjustly betray him? Yes. But he chose to forgive. When his brothers came to see him he had the power to have them killed or enslaved with the flick of the wrist. Some of us would have sulked in our bedchamber, replaying the injustice over and over in our mind. Not Joseph. Remember what he named his sons? "I have forgotten," and "Life is better than I ever hoped." He had forgiven. When his brothers reentered his life, he went back into his pain with courage and boldness and relived his story using a new set of emotional and spiritual tools. He gave himself and his brothers another chance at a relationship.

An obvious question here is: What if Judah and the others hadn't changed?

What if they were just as conniving and evil as before?

Would Joseph have responded the same way?

What we discover in Joseph's motives is not a vengeful spirit, but quite the opposite. He sought reconciliation and went to great lengths to help those who hurt him deal with their own guilt and shame. Regardless of how the brothers may or may not have responded, it seems Joseph discovered a great truth described here by Philip Yancey: "By forgiving another, I am trusting that God is a better justice-maker than I am. By forgiving, I release my own right to get even and leave all issues of fairness for God to work out. I leave in God's hands the scales that must balance justice and mercy."[29]

This is the great irony. It is the forgiving people who have the real authority and confidence.

Unforgiveness offers only a pseudo feeling of power.

We say, "I hold something over you because of what you did to me."

All the while, that person, alive or dead, holds the power because we are the ones who are locked up! Life is sucked from you while you stare at the scales, judging whose sin is weightier than your own: "Whenever someone wrongs you, you caricature them in your heart, making huge their worst feature. Deep in every human soul is a deep desire to justify yourself. We're afraid that we're not okay, that we're not desirable. That fear is behind how you caricature the person who wrongs you. You need to feel noble, you need to feel superior, you need to feel better."[30]

Demeaning the personhood of another fictitiously elevates us, and judging another leaves us full of arrogance, entitlement, and unforgiveness. "Playing God" in judging someone's motives only infuses us with an increasingly cancerous preoccupation with self that sends us plummeting into the abyss of perceived superiority or the fears of possible inferiority.

We chain ourselves to the dock, watching the life of adventure sail on without us. It is self-imposed imprisonment. We think there is so much power in unforgiveness, when the reality is we live as the forlorn castaway, powerless and pitiful.

- We tend to think this world is about us. But our story, in the expanse of history, is nothing but a vignette, a small picture with blurred edges, a brief journal entry. Life is really about another story. When we can begin to see the commonality in our species, when we acknowledge that we are all broken yet redeemed for a higher purpose, when we get that, we forgive. As my father has reminded me often, the ground is level at the foot of the cross.

As Angie and I continued to forgive each other and trust God, He continued to strip away the lies and reveal truth. Angie sent me an email in early September of 2009 that fell deeply on my soul:

Jamie,

I wanted you to know that I am so thankful for you. I can't imagine the pressure you carry. I hurt for you last night when you said that it sucks to constantly disappoint people. (As Doyle says, "It is a reminder of the pain of the fall.") I think once you said that, it brought a lot of things into perspective for me. I hate that I have played a part in making you feel that way. I know I will be disappointed, but I will try to communicate only what the Spirit wants me to. My desire is to not put unnecessary pressure on you, a burden you weren't designed to carry. Remember ... we all are sometimes forced into situations in order for us to see how our "unmet longings" guide us to find Him. I believe people desire to be with you because of how you make them feel ... for them it's a "taste" of what it feels like sitting with Jesus—and yet our lives aren't meant to satisfy people's thirst, just to be a taste of what it is like sitting at Jesus' feet. You are an amazing pastor, father, friend, and husband. Our kids love you deeply. You are a man who follows hard after God, and I am so thankful that God has allowed me to be the person who gets to walk alongside you. "Let us not become weary in doing good, for at the proper time we will reap a harvest if we do not give up" (Gal. 6:9).

I love you,
Angie

When I received this email from Angie, I felt hope rise within me. I felt loved and whole. Her kind words lighted on me in a soft and gentle way.

Though her words continure to be very meaningful to me, I realize I still have work to do when it comes to receiving. There is a vulnerability and humility in allowing words of affirmation to seep in. While my tendency is to see the best in everyone else, I am often critical of myself, allowing my shortcomings to rise to the surface. I was and still am learning that *not* receiving becomes an unkind response to the one who offers the gift. I do not serve my wife well when I quickly diffuse or disparage words of affirmation. There is something trusting and life-giving in the simple words *thank you.*

Angie had forgiven me. I had forgiven Angie. Neither of us held on to our pseudo power over the other. There is a freedom in forgiving and being forgiven.

There is a ship waiting to sail. The Captain has welcomed you aboard for a spectacular voyage. The taste of the salty sea air on your lips, the wind caressing your face, the anticipation of discovery—if you stay on shore, chained to the dock, you will never feel or experience these things.

Look down. Look close. There is a key at your feet. On that key is inscribed a word: *forgive.*

The Captain is motioning, calling, and inviting you into the adventure. His voice is distant, almost a whisper, but you understand. His words are simple and invitational: "Use the key, and come away with me."

    1. Stuck? Say it. Acknowledge it. Open your eyes.

    2. Stuck? Do something new. Find resistance and push through it.

3. Stuck? Eliminate distractions. Create space and feel.

4. Stuck? Identify the obstacle. Speak out shame.

5. Stuck? Set boundaries. Learn to say no.

6. Stuck? Recognize the value of suffering. Feel through your pain.

7. Stuck? Listen to someone else's story. Be vulnerable with yours.

8. Stuck? Take inventory. List what you have learned.

9. Stuck? Forgive. Stay open to connection.

Chapter 10

LOVE LONGS TO BE KNOWN

Love is the measure by which life will be assessed.[1]

Dan Allender and Tremper Longman III

He meant us to see Him and live with Him
and draw our life from His smile.[2]

A. W. Tozer

One evening after getting the kids to bed and watching *Parenthood*, a fascinating television show of love and dysfunction, Angie looked over at me and mused, "You know, we haven't had an argument in months."

"Wow. You're right."

Angie smirked. "Aren't you glad I'm not ready with a current evaluation of our marriage?"

"I suppose I've done a lousy job of affirming you for that." I laughed.

She smiled back. "You sure have."

We talked about how blessed we were that things had changed. Here we were laughing with each other about our own insufficiency.

I looked at Angie. "You know, many relationships don't end up this way. Why are we so fortunate?"

"We didn't give up. We invited people into our story. We had a lot of people who were there for us, encouraging and praying for us."

I nodded. "You know you led the way, going to Doyle and refusing to settle. Thank you for always searching for truth."

Angie leaned in. "Well, that was nice."

"Yeah, still working on getting my thoughts off the production line and onto the truck."

For Angie and me, this little exchange was a beautiful and healthy display of love one toward the other. If you were to spin the diamond on the moment, flirting, confession, affirmation, vulnerability, curiosity, longing, mystery, and creativity would reflect back.

For us, this was love.

LOVE IS A MANY-SPLENDORED THING

Try this. Write down your definition of love.

Yesterday, whom did you love well? How did you know it was love? Who loved *you* well yesterday, and how did you know it was love?

Isn't it interesting that the Bible instructs us to love over and over but doesn't give us a whole lot of specifics? "Love is the most context-specific act in the entire spectrum of human behavior.... Every act of love requires creative and personal giving, responding, and serving appropriate to—context specific to—both the person doing the loving and the person being loved."[3]

The way I love my children is context specific. Sometimes while we're sitting in a restaurant, waiting for our food, I'll ask our youngest one, Addie, why she has laugh buttons. Then I'll start pushing them. She laughs while I tickle her.

Imagine if I used the same approach to display love to my twin boys, who are seniors in high school.

"Son, do you have a laugh button?"

One of them would look at me inquisitively and give me an elbow to the face.

Love is context specific. When the boys have a friend over and need a fourth person for *Call of Duty*, and I willingly suppress my ego by being repeatedly destroyed by three adolescent boys—that, I tell you, is an act of love.

When my daughter Ashton, who is a freshman and very ready to begin dating, defers her preferences and trusts her father, that is an act of love. (I told her—somewhat tongue-in-cheek—she could begin dating when she was a senior, and she negotiated me down to her sophomore year. She is counting the days.) My daughter is beautiful, and trusting her (eventually) to *any* teenage boy? Act of love.

Love is not a formula. And love does not exist in the abstract. Love is rooted in reality.

One day while walking across a parking lot, Addie, at the time five years old, declared to me, "I know that you're in love with Mommy. Wanna know how?"

Angie and I were holding hands in front of her. We glanced over our shoulders and asked, "How?"

"'Cause you grab her butt," Addie replied with a hearty chuckle. They say the last kid always grows up a bit quicker.

Love is tangible. We see it in a smile, a meal, a hug, or an affectionate touch. People are involved. You have to enter into a relationship for it to be expressed or received: "Love is handing your heart to someone and taking the risk that they will hand it back because they don't want it.... Love is a giving away of power.... We expose ourselves.... Love is giving up control. It's surrendering the desire to control the other person."[4]

LOVE IS IMMEASURABLE

I had a discussion with a pastor friend of mine recently. He said he had changed.

He had learned the hard way not to trust people. He said he would be vulnerable with his wife and his wife only.

I wonder how that works. What would it be like for a church to never catch a true glimpse of their pastor's heart? And how do you control the outcome of a relationship on its outset?

It would seem that you would manage everything about your interactions from the first moment you meet someone. To me that sounds like controlling a commodity, not loving a human being.

That same day, I had lunch with a young man from our church. He told me his story, including the recent tragic death of his brother. They had been rock climbing, and his brother fell to his death. We both shed tears as he described the experience.

I felt loved by him. He trusted me enough to pour out his heart. And I felt love for him. My heart went out to him as I entered the story. I felt compassion and hope and admiration. A few months later he moved out West, and we lost touch. But for a moment in time, we experienced a connection. I was invited to live and feel in his story, and I would not be the same because of it.

I believe the reason we stop leaning in with openness is because we are afraid.

Afraid of being hurt.

Forgotten.

Abandoned.

Sometimes we are afraid that our affection for another might be deeper than their affection for us. We start measuring, wondering if the love exchange is equitable.

Doyle once explained to Angie and me that it is not very often that our love, if it could be measured, would be found evenly distributed. There would be moments we would both equally feel a sense of euphoric love for each other, and there would be times when our feelings would not be aligned.

This was freeing for both of us.

From her great assimilation of marriage how-to books, Angie had developed a misunderstanding that we should both feel the exact same way about each other all day, every day. She had in her mind a marriage utopia and was dedicated to its realization. I followed her instruction, and we both lived long, frantic stretches out of emotional breath, straining to somehow sync up.

There is no fear in love. But perfect love drives out fear.[5]

John the apostle

When we love well, we are not preoccupied with uniformity.

"Where there is love there are no demands, no expectations, no dependency.

I do not demand that you make me happy: my happiness does not lie in you.

If you were to leave me, I will not feel sorry for myself;

I enjoy your company, but I do not cling.

I enjoy it on a nonclinging basis.

What I really enjoy is not you;

it's something that's greater than both you and me.

It is something discovered, a kind of symphony, a kind of orchestra that plays one melody in your presence, but when you depart, the orchestra doesn't stop.

When I meet someone else, it plays another melody, which is also very delightful. And when I'm alone, it continues to play."[6]

INVITATION ONLY

Through our journey and Doyle's guidance, Angie and I discovered what it meant to see the other first not as our spouse, but as an individual placed on the earth as God's child. While Angie is my wife; she is first my sister in God's family. I am Angie's husband, but first her brother in God's family. Through this, my wife learned to express her desires without the expectation of demand; I learned to look beneath her words and see her heart.

I am writing this in a hotel room in Los Angeles. I officiated a wedding for our good friends Joel and Moriah just south of here a few days ago. Angie was supposed to come with me to be a part of the festivities, and then we were going to spend a couple of days celebrating our anniversary.

Our family was in New York just prior to the trip to California. On our way home, our Suburban broke down somewhere in northern Ohio. It limped along until we made it to Cincinnati. I called my friend Ivo, who gathered some friends, rescued us, and took us to a car rental agency just as it was closing. (We got pulled over by the police for speeding to get there on time.) There were no large vehicles at the facility, so we were forced to rent two cars to drive home to Tennessee, meaning Angie had to drive one of them in the pouring rain for five hours in the middle of the night. We arrived at our house around two o'clock in the morning to discover mice in our kitchen and a possum in our basement. There was more. A flea colony had taken up residence outside our back door, and our dog started having allergic reactions to the fleas and apparently every food group and fabric made in the Western hemisphere. (If you ever want to rescue a dog, avoid cocker spaniels.) Needless to say, Angie, who had been planning on going to LA with me the next morning, hit the eject button and decided to leave earth. I mean, stay home.

In the past, when circumstances were seemingly out of control, I would have tried to fix everything. In the past, Angie would have been caught in a tailspin, stressed out and lost in unmet expectations.

Here is what is new for us. While feeling her disappointment, Angie started solving the problems at home and moved easily through them. Since we were unable to be together on the West Coast, she sent me a text asking, "I desire that you would plan something for our anniversary, maybe Thursday through Saturday? Stay somewhere in town?"

No demand.

No manipulation.

A meaningful desire posed in a question.

Freedom.

Space.

Not duty, but desire swells within me to meet Angie's desires and my own. I want to spend time together too. I want to be with her and display love for her. I want to appreciate her sacrifice and willingness to give up something she was looking forward to in order to hold down the fort at home.

This is how God loves us. No demand. No manipulation. Freedom. Space.

Rather than force Himself on us, He invites us into a relationship with Him. He can't help it. Love longs to be known. That is the nature of a God-like love: "God is love. Whoever lives in love lives in God, and God in them."[7]

If God is love, then by His very nature He must offer Himself to someone. While I have trouble comprehending it, I believe this is why God must exist in a Trinitarian form. If God is love, then that love must always be expressed. If I sat and stared at pictures of my wife and children and never interacted with them, I would not experience connection. Without engaging in relationship, I am deprived of love.

In the Trinity, love has been exchanged perfectly for all eternity. This must have happened before something was created, for if something was created, it would not be God. If it was not God, then it was not love. Therefore, God had to exist in relationship.

I am often asked, "If God is love, why is there so much injustice in the world?" While this is an important question and a difficult one to answer, consider this: for love to exist, choice must exist. Love would cease to be love if it was forced. Thus the other must choose. Accept or reject.

A RETURN TO LOVE

In order to have choice, something other than good must exist. The contrast to good, of course, is evil.

Evil was introduced before the creation of man. God created a being different from humans. Angels, while immensely powerful, are not created in God's image. It seems that in God's heavenly design, He allowed this race of beings to exist, and one-third of those to rebel, instigating a contrast to His love.

Full of pride, the leader of this band of rebels, Lucifer, became the ever-present villain in our story. He hates God. Hates love. He deceived our ancestors, pulling them away from uninhibited companionship with God.

We are now on a quest to return to that perfect communion.

God did not create relationship. It has always existed. In perfect intimacy. Every longing fulfilled. Continually, in ongoing celebration.

The model of what that perfect intimacy is like for mankind? Marriage. And in the context of marriage, the closest example to what perfect intimacy is like? Sexual union, peaking at climax for just a moment. Only to leave us remembering afterward that on this side of heaven, all is temporary.

The properly and lovingly executed and
mutually satisfying sexual union is God's way of
demonstrating to us a great spiritual truth.[8]

Ed and Gaye Wheat

Man and woman are the only creatures that engage in sexuality face-to-face. This is not just sex with a body but with a person. There is an exchange happening. Sexuality is designed as part of a bigger picture, as is everything created by God. And while sexuality seems to be the zenith of human intimacy, it is but a shadow of what our eternal intimacy with God has been created to be.

God is writing a love story: man's return to wholeness, an eternal satisfaction found only in return to a love relationship with his Creator God.

In our fractured state, intimacy seems tied only to moments.

It finds itself caught in the constraints of time.

In the confines of a broken world, a fallen humanity.

We are left with a constant longing for more.

God has designed all of creation to push glory His way. To remind us that there is an epic story unraveling, that we have been created for something more than we are now. He has placed in the creation rhythms signs, whispers, and reminders that we are not whole and that there is something more.

THE LOVING FATHER

Jesus left us with a marvelous example of a loving father. Luke, the good doctor-turned-journalist, records this story from Jesus in the fifteenth chapter of his self-titled book:

> There was a man who had two sons. The younger one said to his father, "Father, give me my share of the estate." So he divided his property between them.
>
> Not long after that, the younger son got together all he had, set off for a distant country and there squandered his wealth in wild living. After he had spent everything, there was a severe famine in that whole country, and he began to be in need. So he went and hired himself out to a citizen of that country, who sent him to his fields to feed pigs. He longed to fill his stomach with the pods that the pigs were eating, but no one gave him anything.
>
> When he came to his senses, he said, "How many of my father's hired servants have food to spare, and here I am starving to death! I will set out and go back to my father and say to him: Father, I have sinned against heaven and against you. I am

> no longer worthy to be called your son; make me
> like one of your hired servants."
>
> So he got up and went to his father.[9]

This is quite a scene. It would have been considered tabloid fare to the crowd that first heard this story. In Middle Eastern culture, speaking this way to your father was an insult. It's like saying, "Father, I cannot wait for you to die."[10] Or, "I want you to put *your* future at risk—give me what is my due." More than just an act of disrespect, it is an act of brutal betrayal.

What is the father's response?

Is he an angry dad with lightning bolts in his fists and a sick and anxious desire to smoke the son who ran off with his money? Or a detective dad, investigating and recording his son's every move, action, and behavior in order to shame, judge, and ultimately shun his son for eternity?

That is not how the story goes.

This was a patient father who knew that it was only by letting his son go that his son would ever have a chance to give love in return.

While officiating wedding ceremonies, I often say this to the couple and their families: "Love is not found in the strength of your grip but in the tenderness of your release."

The father knows that more information is not going to change his son. A lecture is not going to provide transformation. His son has to find something, and he has to find it on his own. Sometimes children have trouble recognizing love. It is not until they go away that they see it for what it is.

COMING HOME

The prodigal child can't see what is in front of him. The truth is, the son doesn't even know what he is looking for. Somewhere deep within he is desperate for perspective. The father understands this. Though it is painful to know his son has to suffer, the father knows that they will both never experience true love until his son realizes, with profound honesty, his need to be in relationship with his loving father.

There is a very important line in this story: "He longed to fill his stomach with the pods that the pigs were eating, but no one gave him anything."[11]

Mr. I-Will-Control-My-Own-Destiny prodigal boy would be content living in the pigsty if he just had *something*! He can't see clearly until he is no longer given *anything*.

If you are like me, you often prevent people from crashing to the bottom because you are always giving them something. Sometimes you run on empty and you have nothing left to give. And you're still giving!

Telegram to all the enablers in the world: You are not the Messiah. Stop. Give people space. Stop.

At his lowest point, completely stripped of his arrogance and self-reliance, the prodigal woke up. He believed. He had faith that his father's love was truly what the father claimed it was. Strong. Forgiving. Compassionate. And patient.

He walked home. He didn't run. Maybe he lacked the strength. Maybe he lacked the confidence. Point is, he started the journey back to his father.

PATIENT LOVE

> So he got up and went to his father. But while he was still a long way off, his father saw him and was filled with compassion for him; he ran to his son, threw his arms around him and kissed him [12]

This scene is perhaps one of my favorites in all of Jesus' stories. It begins with this line: "But while he was still a long way off."

What does this tell us about the father? What does it tell us about God?

He never stops waiting.

He sits on the porch. It's a sunny day. On the table next to him, beads of moisture glide down a glass of lemonade. He looks up. He leans forward. There is a man, emaciated, wearing nothing but tattered pants, stumbling up the path to the front gate.

But there is something about his posture ... something about the way he walks.

The father leaps from his chair, knocking over the table, his glass full of lemonade falling and spilling out over the porch. He skips a step, jumping down to the sidewalk in a full sprint toward the front gate. His heart burns, his throat burdened by a rising lump. His eyes start to sting from the tears fighting their way to the surface. The father throws open the gate and hugs his son so hard and so fast he almost knocks the wind out of him. He lifts his son from the ground and buries his head in his shoulder.

The son is overwhelmed, unprepared for this kind of display of affection. The smell of his father's skin, the tickle of his whiskers on his cheek—so warm, so loving. His mind is instantly flooded with memories from his childhood, a larger-than-life daddy who read him stories and made him laugh and picked him up when he fell.

Suddenly, the memories are cut off like a TV signal that goes dead.

The next image that appears is his father's face the day he told his father he could not care less about his own dreams and demanded that he be given what he deserved. The day he uttered those life-altering words "I hate you."

His father, in the face of hatred, had willingly given him all that he asked for.

The son can feel what little energy he has left quickly vanishing. He pushes his father away, grabbing the gate for stability. He had rehearsed a speech, and with the memories bearing down on him, now more than ever, he must be clear about his expectations.

"Father, I have sinned against heaven and against you. I am no longer worthy to be called your son."[13] He is broken. He is sorry. He has known how to love only in a limited way. The reach of his imagination stops at the possibility of joining the family help.

> But the father said to his servants, "Quick! Bring the best robe and put it on him. Put a ring on his finger and sandals on his feet. Bring the fattened calf and kill it. Let's have a feast and celebrate. For this son of mine was dead and is alive again; he was lost and is found." So they began to celebrate.[14]

His father seems to not even hear the rehearsed speech. He quickly calls a servant and asks for clothes. He also wants a signet ring, an identifying symbol of family, rushed out as well. The father's final instruction is to throw a party, a feast in honor of his son's return.

Here is the overwhelming truth: this is a wild love.

A love difficult to comprehend and more unsettling, a love we are unable to restrain. The flesh, the broken part of our humanity, longs to be in command, longs to be able to identify finite lines of understanding so that we can master that understanding, feel safe, and be in control. The love of this father is anything but safe and predictable.

There is an oft-quoted line from *The Lion, the Witch and the Wardrobe* in which Mr. Beaver is responding to young Lucy's question about Aslan, the God-character in the story:

> "He isn't safe?" said Lucy.

> "Safe?" said Mr. Beaver; "Who said anything about safe? 'Course he isn't safe. But he's good. He's the King, I tell you."[15]

God is passionately in love with you. Allow your imagination to stretch to its furthest reach, and then tell yourself you have barely passed your rooftop. There is an entire universe and beyond that can hardly contain the love that is waiting for you.

Stop trying to experience love on your own terms, and open yourself up to God. When you do, when you allow yourself to be truly known, you will discover within you a compulsion to give love away like you have never known.

Love longs to be known. It is in that knowing and being known that we learn to love well.

1. Stuck? Say it. Acknowledge it. Open your eyes.

2. Stuck? Do something new. Find resistance and push through it.

3. Stuck? Eliminate distractions. Create space and feel.

4. Stuck? Identify the obstacle. Speak out shame

5. Stuck? Set boundaries. Learn to say no.

6. Stuck? Recognize the value of suffering. Feel through your pain.

7. Stuck? Listen to someone else's story. Be vulnerable with yours.

8. *Stuck? Take inventory. List what you have learned.*

9. *Stuck? Forgive. Stay open to connection.*

10. *Stuck? Receive love. Give yourself away.*

Chapter 11

JOY-FULL

Great joy depends upon first having carried great tension.[1]
Ronald Rolheiser

The fruit of the Spirit is ... joy.[2]
Paul the apostle

As we receive and give love away we begin experiencing an emotion that we had forgotten about. Joy.

Wow. That's what that is.

A smile breaks out across your face before you realize it.

Laughter emits effortlessly, and you haven't even had any wine.

Something has changed.

You hear the birds harmonizing in the morning and the crickets playing their song at night.

The sun kisses your skin and the breeze combs your hair.

There it is. You are smiling again.

Wait, was that a skip?

Did you just playfully punch a coworker?

Did you just jog to get the mail?

Were you whistling?

Did a lyric from a Top 40 hit from high school leap from your tongue?

Did you just chuckle while picturing a youth pastor sprinting triumphantly until a wall emerged in the twilight, abruptly ending his capture-the-flag euphoria?

What is happening to you?

Joy.

You have turned in your badge as chief operations officer of the universe.

You love yourself today.

You love others today.

You are loved by God and love Him in return.

> *We are invited to rejoice in every moment of life*
> *because every moment of life is a gift.*[3]
>
> John Ortberg

Hopefully as you get unstuck, as you experience the beauty of love, you discover that life can be truly good and satisfying. Each moment is a gift, if we but dare enjoy it in its sacred simplicity.

In chapter 1, I mentioned two songwriters, my friends David and Leslie. Together we lead our church through a worship experience each week. Often we sing songs suffused with deep reflection and lament—and that is good, as we have been invited by God to confess our profound need for Him. However, one day after finally sitting down to write together, I mentioned my desire to write a song that speaks of the peaceful, pleasant joy that comes from simply being in the moment.

So together in a small studio in the back of Building 8 in The Factory (where our church gathers) we did just that.

We are all stumbling
Struggling to find our feet
Fumbling toward something sweet
Just breathing in

Looking up for something clear
Knowing what's ahead is near
Holding on to faith not fear
Just breathing in

Your love is
So pleasant so safe so sound

We are all running free
Carried by Your grace and peace
Living for eternity
We're breathing in

Your love is
So pleasant so safe so sound

You're dangerous but liberating
You're furious but still redeeming
You follow us but still You're leading
You are so faithfully wondrous

Your love is
So pleasant so safe so sound.[4]

JOY—A STATE OF BEING

When we realize that we are moving again, life gets lighter. We walk a bit slower, listen a little longer. We get better at being fully present.

Our demeanor changes. Some of life's intensity slides away, and we feel the pleasantness of love.

Moments have meaning again.

Angie and I recently celebrated our twentieth wedding anniversary. Wonderful friends offered their beach house in Florida so we could get away for a week. During that time, we experienced a freedom with each other we hadn't known since the early days of our marriage. Angie was completely in the moment. No evaluation. No expectations. I was attentive and shared thoughts and feelings freely. We sat and read together, were intimate, and enjoyed just being with each other

It was the first trip without an argument that either of us could remember.

Angie says she finally experienced what had been so elusive throughout her last decade: contentment. I asked if she remembered when she first felt this state of being. She immediately talked about her trip to a monastery, where she spent contemplative time in isolation. (Think back to chapter 2.) Angie doesn't like to be alone, so going to a Catholic retreat center and living in silence for three days was a significant stretch. But she did it.

At dusk one evening at the monastery, after sitting outside in meditation near a pond, Angie looked up. The dramatic scene unfolding over the sanctuary was mesmerizing. The sky was translucent with colors that danced playfully with one another. She immediately sensed God's presence. She smiled. No angst. No struggle. Just joy. In that moment, Angie told me, the beautiful display of artistic wonder felt like it was a gift designed just for her.

> *This is the day that the LORD has made;*
> *let us rejoice and be glad in it.*[5]
>
> A Hebrew psalm

Joy is defined as "the emotion of great delight or happiness caused by something exceptionally good or satisfying; keen pleasure; elation."[6]

To live in never-ending delight was a part of our original design. However, this is challenging for us. I like what Ronald Rolheiser says: "In Western culture, the joyous shouting of children often irritates us because it interferes with our depression. That is why we have invented a term, hyperactivity, so that we can, in good conscience, sedate the spontaneous joy in many of our children."[7]

I have a mentor in my life whom I would describe as a man of joy.

His name is Dr. Albert Lemmons. He is seventy-seven years young.

He is not stressed.

He is not frustrated with the way people drive.

He is not filled with angst about the direction of the government.

He is not constantly irritated with people who fail to meet his expectations.

Our conversations are often interrupted by his tears or by his spontaneous prayer.

Tears, because it occurs to him how thankful he is, and prayer as he immediately passes on the burden of whatever is at hand to his Father.

Dr. Lemmons has taught me something through the way he experiences life.

He knows how to just be. He can do this because he takes God at His word.

Joy is expressed in trusting.

Every moment is confronted with this question:

Is God trustworthy?

If we answer no, then we must pursue control. We must manage people and circumstances. We must exist in an ever-present state of fear and distrust, for that is the only way we will survive. After all, if you can't trust God, who can you trust?

If God is, in fact, trustworthy; *enjoy Him*!

> *Rejoice in the Lord always; again I will say, rejoice.*[8]
>
> Paul the apostle

Take in the moments.

Stop to smell the roses. Literally stop. Smell the roses.

Notice the little graces and take pleasure in them. Take in the colors of the sky, the peace reflected on the face of your sleeping child, the knowing glance from your spouse, the flutter in your heart for the one you wait to see enter the class-room, the colors on the prairie, the smell of fresh-cut grass, the sound of creaking wood on the country bridge, the silence of a winter's day, the red letters in your Bible that speak of a love that overwhelms the world.

"How many activities can you count in your life that you engage in simply because they delight you and grip your soul? Find them out, cultivate them, for they are your passport to freedom and to love."[9]

It is of the LORD's mercies that we are not consumed, because his compassions fail not. They are new every morning.[10]

Jeremiah the prophet

Your world is flooded with gifts! And joy begins to well up as it becomes difficult to comprehend the magnitude of God's generosity.

CELEBRATION

I have a favorite moment in the Christmas classic *White Christmas* with Bing Crosby and Rosemary Clooney. Bing's character, Bob Wallace, is an entertainer who is staying at an old inn run by a retired general whom he served under during the war. Bob's business partner and fellow showman is trying to get Bob hitched. Though Bob is resistant at first, a romance ignites between Bob and Betty (Clooney's character), a singer in the show he is producing. One night Bob can't sleep, and he heads to the kitchen for a glass of milk. It seems Betty can't sleep either. She comes to the kitchen as well and shares her difficulty with Bob. He sings her a song that reveals the cure to his insomnia: instead of counting sheep, he counts his blessings.

Sleep deprived or not, this is a good idea.

Try this. Begin writing, without filtering, what blessings exist in your life.

Seriously. Pick up a pen and start writing.

Begin with: "I currently have access to oxygen."

Then try, "Thank You for creating the color green." (If you are color blind, count it a blessing you will never have to look at the color goldenrod. Trust me.)

No blessing is too small. Write until you fill up the page.

What you are doing when you are writing is actually celebrating.

Celebration is delighting in something, and more specifically someone, outside of us. It is giving attention to someone and speaking of that person's worth.

My aunt Sally was into celebrating. To her, it was an art form. And it always involved food. She lived in a small house in the city of Buffalo, New York. She cooked in a tiny kitchen without air conditioning. During the summers when my family went over to celebrate a holiday or birthday, we would go up the stairs and enter the house through her kitchen. She was always the first to greet us. Her hands were usually sticky with a culinary masterpiece in progress, and the perspiration from the unavoidable heat in her home caused her glasses to continually slide halfway down her nose. Avoiding her dough-battered fingers and falling glasses, my childish face would glide across her sweaty cheeks, and her forearm would squeeze me close.

Whether we were celebrating God, our country, or one another, the day was filled with food and laughter. I'm not sure my sisters, cousins, or I will ever be able to replicate those moments.

When I think back to those times, my heart is flooded with joy. It seems that those from previous generations, before the advent of fast food, intuitively knew something about the connection between food and meaningful relationship. Good food is never fast. It takes time and attention.

It requires creativity and conversation. And when it is time to eat, everyone must cease to be productive.

Maybe that is the point—we are forced to slow, if even for a moment.

Something else is obvious at the table—we are all equally dependent. The need for food reminds us that we are but frail creatures who, without nourishment, cannot survive very long on this third rock from the sun. The very act of moving food from our plate to our mouth displays that we are not sufficient unto ourselves. For a moment, however brief, we are humbled. While the food fills our bellies, gratitude should fill our souls.

There is a temptation to say, "Sure. I get it. I know I need to celebrate. I'll get around to it at some point. I just don't have time right now."

When my mother gets better,

When my schedule slows down,

When I get in shape,

When I pay off my debt,

When I find a girlfriend ...

Then, for sure, I will take the time to be happy.

Maybe. You might. For a few moments.

And while happiness is a good virtue to pursue, it seems fastened to moments. Joy, however, is like a liquid. When it hits, you get drenched.

Joy is an attitude. A disposition of the heart. It's about being open to and seeing goodness. Without this we remain stuck in our self-absorption.

The more spacious and larger our fundamental
nature, the more bearable the pains of living.

Wayne Muller

If you fail to celebrate people and life, your attitude will naturally drift toward critique.

Most people can handle critique only in small doses. If you
live as the omniscient pessimist, people will eventually avoid
being around you.

There was a young man in our church who felt he had been
victimized by most of the people in his life. He led every conversation with indictment on the church, on God, and on the
human race in general. Angie and I invited him over for dinner
one evening. We hoped it would be meaningful for him to sit at
a table and be immersed in a loving, boisterous family dynamic.
When we finished the meal, and as soon as he had me in a
corner, he launched into his tirade of criticism. Anger and bitterness spewed from him like a fire hose without its master.

I looked over his shoulder for a moment and could see my
kids (young at the time) at play. Addie was crawling around,
playing with toys and squealing. Ashton sat at the table,
coloring, and the boys were going back and forth between
tackling each other and playing football on a video game.
Here he stood, in a room where joy was swirling all around
him, and he could see none of it. All he could see was a

planet full of degenerate people. His self-loathing could not be concealed.

He left our home with an odor from the brackish puddles of his hatred. We prayed for him and for a swift breeze.

How very sad.

I have come to believe that goodness of some variety is always nearby. The question is always whether we have eyes to see and ears to hear. Will we remain awake long enough to recognize the rich textures of life that surround our every movement?

OPEN YOURSELF TO GOODNESS

One of the questions Angie and her friends in her village ask themselves each week is, "What is good in your life?" This question prompts celebration, which produces a sense of gratitude. Before these women focus on struggles and challenges, they are reminded of God's goodness and generosity. Joy emerges as they spend time together.

Relationships are inconvenient. So is brushing your teeth.

Don't take time for it, and eventually you will see the results.

Spirit carriers evoke joy from their energy. You can't help but want to be around them. Terry and Susie are my spiritual Red

Bull. I met them about five years ago when they stumbled onto our motley crew and were immediately intrigued. They were in their fifties and hadn't been to a church in thirty-seven years.

Terry was a retired engineer. Susie, a writer. They introduced themselves one Sunday.

Terry said he couldn't wrap his mind around the kind of God I had just described. Susie said that much of what I talked about just made her mad.

They kept coming.

Over the course of the next two years, they would occasionally find me after a service. Terry would shrug his shoulders and say he needed more proof that a loving and fair God truly existed. Susie would tell me she didn't know "what the hell" I was talking about. They would both give me a hug and say, "I guess we'll see you next week."

One night at our church Christmas party, Terry walked up to me and said, "Well, pastor, I got on my knees last night and gave my life to God. I have been lost in my head and have decided to engage my heart." He paused. "But I don't really want you to tell anyone."

"Okay." I nodded, smiling from ear to ear, my eyes a little teary. "I'm excited about the journey ahead for you."

Within a few months Terry and Susie asked if they could start a library for people who were interested in the books I quoted from during my Sunday talks. Terry, who hadn't read a book completely in over twenty years, was now devouring them. The one he enjoyed most was called the Bible, a book I am particularly fond of.

Fast-forward another year. Terry and Susie asked to be baptized. Terry said, "I have to tell everyone!" The waters of baptism are symbolic of a water grave. Terry and Susie had been walking around dead but had been raised to life. Baptism was their megaphone to the world. They had an announcement to make: they had fallen completely in love with Jesus.

Today, their library at church keeps growing. Terry loves talking to atheist engineers. And Susie asks people analyzing God for too long what the hell are they waiting for.

Finding Jesus wasn't simple for these two people. It didn't happen overnight. But with countless hours of relationship exchange with others in our church, Terry and Susie went from analytical skeptics to ambassadors of joy.

I saw them both this morning. Susie put her arm around me and said,

"I can't imagine life without God."

I can't imagine life without Terry and Susie.

This couple is so full of life that it overflows and splashes on those around them.

There are life givers and life suckers.

Suggestion: be intentional with those you choose to spend time with.

It might be helpful to offer a clarification here regarding how joy is sometimes misinterpreted. Some people come across as bubbly and bouncy and say, "Bless your heart," at the end of their sentences. This is not necessarlly joy.

It might be.

And it might not.

Some people present themselves as pervasively happy because they are exceedingly afraid.

They are so terrified of conflict that they keep the upper hand by making everything seem as if you are on *Mr. Rogers' Neighborhood*. If they keep a sweater nearby and talk to creepy puppets, I suggest you change the relational channel. Trust your instincts on this. If people seem fake, they probably are. Joy is never forced; it is the liquid that flows freely.

THE CHIEF END OF MAN

Certain Protestant Christians have held to a particular creed for the past four hundred years. It comes from the *Westminster Shorter Catechism* of the 1640s: "Man's chief end is to glorify God, and to enjoy him forever."

This is a central statement in Christianity, so why does it seem that so many fail to enjoy God? It seems many who claim to follow Jesus are bored and depressed. If this creed is to be lived out, then Jesus followers must concede that there is an adventure to be had. Erwin McManus calls this the Barbarian Way:

> Barbarians are not welcome among the civilized and are feared among the domesticated. The way of Jesus is far too savage for their sensibilities. The sacrifice of God's Son, the way of the Cross, the call to die to ourselves, all lack the dignity of a refined faith…. Our redemption will only come if we find the courage to escape the prison we have created for ourselves. Risking everything to live free is our only hope—humanity's only hope.[11]

Our church, our collection of barbarians, meets in an old factory that has been restored and redeemed. Much of our music is reflective and honest. My goal in teaching is to present truth in story and be honest and authentic about my own journey. Our lights are low, and the creative elements are designed to be a subtle amplification of worship. I suppose this combination may create an atmosphere that lends itself to "feeling," but more than that I believe it is the people who have found their way to Journey who facilitate a spirit of passion and joy.

We are an eclectic collection of broken humans overwhelmed by grace. We have left our chains on the dock and are in a passionate pursuit of new worlds. Our hearts are full, and we are compelled to worship someone greater than ourselves. We funnel that gratitude toward God.

"For it is from the overflow of the heart that the mouth speaks."[12]

TRUE WORSHIP

Praise is often misunderstood. Especially in a church.

If this has been weird for you, you are in good company.

Listen to what the famous philosopher and author C. S. Lewis has to say:

> When I first began to draw near to belief in God
> and even for some time after it had been given to

me, I found a stumbling block in the demand so
clamorously made by all religious people that we
should "praise" God; still more in the suggestion
that God Himself demanded it. We all despise the
man who demands continued assurance of his
own virtue, intelligence, or delightfulness....

The most obvious fact about praise—whether of
God or anything—strangely escaped me. I thought
of it in terms of compliment, approval, or the giving
of honour. I had never noticed that all enjoyment
spontaneously overflows into praise.... The world
rings with praise—lovers praising their mistresses,
readers praising their favourite poet, walkers praising the countryside, players praising their favourite
game—praise of weather, wines, dishes, actors.... I
had not noticed how the humblest, and at the same
time most balanced and capacious, minds, praised
most, while the cranks, misfits, and malcontents
praised least.... Praise almost seems to be inner
health made audible.[13]

I have played on many sports teams through the years. An
unwritten rule is that after you win a game, you are supposed
to go out as a team, eat, drink, and talk about how awesome
you are. Whether your contribution was routine or game
changing, the experience wouldn't be complete without
some form of praise.

We are compelled to praise because it adds to or finishes the sense of enjoyment.

So if we do not praise God, we don't complete our enjoyment of Him.

It's like being married and never making love.

Or watching a great film and never commenting on it.

Or watching your team win the Super Bowl in the last seconds and casually crossing your legs and asking for someone to please pass the cheese dip.

Something would be missing. And you would know it.

Living in Nashville, we have many musicians, authors, and entertainers involved in our church community. Being a person of note is both a blessing and a curse. As Bill Murray quipped, "I always like to say to people who want to be rich and famous, try being rich first…. See if that doesn't cover most of it."[14]

What most fans can't comprehend is how many people entertainers meet. They meet thousands and thousands of people. The average person does not have a brain physiologically designed to contain that many names and faces. So when a fan walks up and references an interaction from years before—like taking the artist to the airport or chatting over a drink or meeting in a line—and then gets upset that the entertainer doesn't remember, that is really unfair. I sometimes hear fans say,

"The reason I want to speak to so-and-so is to encourage them."

Being on both sides of the stage, this is what I have discovered:

(a) the interaction probably did little for them, and

(b) the claim of wanting to "encourage them" probably isn't true.

An example. I was backstage at the Grand Ole Opry a few years ago when a famous young country singer was inducted into the Country Music Hall of Fame. She was standing a few feet away, chatting with friends about the excitement of the evening. Had I interrupted the conversation and said, "Hey, I just wanted you to know that you have an absolutely amazing voice. I'm inspired every time you sing!" what would her response have been?

She is a sweet woman, and I am sure she would have responded politely and said, "Thank you," before swiftly returning to her conversation.

Would my expression of praise have been hugely meaningful to her? Probably not.

Annoying? Good chance.

Would it have been meaningful to me? You bet.

I would have finished off the enjoyment.

My point is that as fans we can have a legitimate desire to speak to someone who has inspired us.

We must accept, however, that most of the time it is for our benefit

If you are welcomed or invited to speak to someone you admire, tell him or her. Don't hesitate. Enjoy the moment. It can be very special.

Just don't force it. And don't place relational expectations on them.

On the flip side, I often remind and encourage entertainers to do their best to be fully present with each fan for that very reason.

If handled appropriately, each is giving a gift to the other.

God tells us to celebrate Him, but not because He needs our affirmation. He is whole and holy unto Himself.

He is not deficient. He is not shallow or insecure, stroking His beard, looking far and wide for people to lavish Him with compliments.

He doesn't pine away in eternity past, struggling to get up each morning because He doesn't have enough human beings around shaking tambourines.

Celebrating God is yet another gift to us.

We are close to concluding our time together. So here's the thing. Take a break. Close the book. Take a walk. Go for a drive. Sit on the roof. Talk to a stranger. Look around.

Is He close? Are you in God's presence?

If you don't sense Him, that's okay. Enjoy the benefit of being included in His story, and keep leaning into the moments with awareness and anticipation.

If, on the other hand, you sense Him nearby, tell Him how you feel about Him. Praise Him.

Finish off the moment.

1. Stuck? Say it. Acknowledge it. Open your eyes.

2. Stuck? Do something new. Find resistance and push through it.

3. Stuck? Eliminate distractions. Create space and feel.

4. Stuck? Identify the obstacle. Speak out shame.

5. Stuck? Set boundaries. Learn to say no.

6. Stuck? Recognize the value of suffering. Feel through your pain.

7. Stuck? Listen to someone else's story. Be vulnerable with yours.

8. Stuck? Take inventory. List what you have learned.

9. Stuck? Forgive. Stay open to connection.

10. Stuck? Receive love. Give yourself away.

11. Stuck? Enjoy life. Celebrate the little things.

Chapter 12

FRAMING REDEMPTION

He simply remains where grace has placed him,
picking up the treasures which lie at his feet.[1]

Hans Urs von Balthasar

The problem of pain meets its match in the scandal of grace.[2]

Philip Yancey

I first saw *Les Misérables* on Broadway in my thirties. Like most of the world, I was taken in by its mystique. It was one of the most inspiring experiences of my life, repeated each time I have seen it performed, and most recently in the musical film version. Years ago, after seeing the live performance, I rented the nonmusical film version starring Liam Neeson and Geoffrey Rush. One of the main characters, Javert, played by Rush, became my favorite person in all of literature. Not because he is good—he is the primary antagonist in the story—but because I am not sure that I have ever seen a character deficiency so profoundly personified. Javert represents moralism, judgment, the law. His way is justice without mercy.

JUDGMENT'S RELENTLESS PURSUIT

With Javert there are no shades of gray, only hard lines of black and white. While hunting the protagonist, whom he has deemed unworthy, Javert offers this in a soliloquy:

> *And if you fall as Lucifer fell, you fall in flames!*
> *And so it must be, for so it is written on the*
> *doorway to Paradise, that those who falter*
> *and those who fall must pay the price!"*[3]

Javert is religion in the worst sense of the word.

He is legalism.

He is arrogant judgment.

He is anger, bitterness, and self-righteousness.

He is a pharisee.

I know him. For I have been him.

I was in high school when I got caught up in moralism. One night my family was heading out to hang with friends. We knew that the parents in that family occasionally enjoyed a beer or glass of wine, but I had been taught that to drink even a drop of alcohol was sin. Before I walked out the front door, I announced to my family that I was going to confront this household about their iniquity. I was particularly perturbed that my parents had not taken the initiative to slow down this runaway train of sin and tomfoolery.

I can still remember my mother yelling to my father, "Richie!"—my mother switched from the casual "Rich" to "Richie" when a child's life was on the line—"You are going to have to do something about your son!" My father made it clear that it was not my place to usher in a new era of Prohibition and made me promise to keep my mouth shut while visiting. I was a dutiful son.

At seventeen, I was working through a litany of my own sins and adolescent struggles, but I could not see them. I saw only what Jesus sarcastically referred to as the speck of sawdust in someone else's eye; I had not noticed the log cabin in my own.[1]

While there have been times when I foolishly judged, I also know what it is like to be tried, criticized, and analyzed. I know what it is like to be hunted by Javert.

And like Jean Valjean, the story's protagonist, I ran. I hid.

In the story, Valjean lives perpetually on the run.

When he was young he was caught stealing a loaf of bread to feed his starving family, and, after trying to escape, his penalty is nineteen years in jail. After being released, he steals again, this time from a priest. He is arrested and confronted by the law, but the priest does something unexpected and life-altering for Valjean. The priest says that the items Valjean took from him were actually a gift. The priest then says he was disappointed because Valjean forgot to take the most expensive of all: a pair of silver candlesticks.

The priest draws close, looks him in the eye, and tells him not to forget what he has been given.

Valjean is dumbfounded. He doesn't know what to make of this kind gesture. He has never experienced compassion of this nature. He realizes in time that what he experienced was more than a good deed.

It was grace.

Undeserved. Yet given freely.

Valjean spends a lifetime serving others while carrying the weight of being pursued by the law. Eventually he comes face-to-face with Javert and has it within his power to kill him. Instead, he gives the law grace.

Valjean's display of grace slowly creates an implosion within Javert. He doesn't know what to do. He cannot reconcile the law and grace. Grace is too powerful for him to control. Life as he knows it ceases to have meaning.

We cannot generate goodness on our own. Even when we think we are altruistic, our impure motives abound. The good that we do in this world comes only from the good that has been first given to us. That good finds its origin in love.

Remember the wild love of the father in chapter 10? It isn't just the younger son who has trouble receiving it. There is an older brother in the story, and he has the same problem.

The father's loving way exists as a stark contrast to his sons' perpetual selfishness.

The younger son runs away to find himself.

The older son stays home to prove himself.

The younger son becomes a hedonist; the older one a moralist.

There is a great tendency to want to prove ourselves to God.

Notice the strife-laden words of the older brother: "Look! All these years I've been slaving for you and never disobeyed your orders."[5]

This is an expression not of love, but of duty.

The older brother has not given love to his father and others, nor has he received love. And since his brother left town with half of the estate, leaving him to do all the work, he wallows in his unforgiveness and self-righteousness.

He is resentful of his brother for leaving, and he is angry with his father for letting him go. Neither his brother nor his father have behaved according to his expectations.

There is an important life principle here. When understanding and empathy are absent, judgment fills the empty space.

It takes only a drop of bitterness to spoil the drink.

How would the story have changed if it were the older brother who met the prodigal at the gate?

The gate would not have been opened.

And a one-sided conversation like this would have ensued:

"You selfish jerk. It looks like you got what you deserved. Who do you think you are? Do you really think you can come back here and just act like nothing happened? You had your chance. You broke your father's heart. We don't love you anymore. Why don't you climb back into whatever hole you came out of?"

These are the words of hate.

This is the response of judgmental religion.

Those who are puffed up in their own knowledge sneer and prance.

This is what we sometimes feel emanating from the person in the seat in front of us, from the lady with the hat, or from the man behind the podium.

Someone shows up at the doors of the church building hoping, maybe, that they can come back to God. Not knowing how. Not even longing for much—just enough patience and compassion to be shown that they can start somewhere.

Unfortunately, it is the older son that many people meet at the gate.

They are shamed for their sin, and looked down upon in their brokenness.

GRACE IS UNFAIR

The moralist older brother doesn't like grace. His brother's arrival has been a devastating eye-opener.

He has played by the rules, and they didn't get him anywhere.

He is exposed. He feels unsafe.

The game he created no longer works in his favor.

The father speaks to his oldest boy: "My son ... you are always with me, and everything I have is yours. But we had to celebrate and be glad, because this brother of yours was dead and is alive again; he was lost and is found."[6]

The father is concerned about one thing above all others.

Life.

Both his sons were the walking dead. Lost, each in his own way.

But one of his boys has confessed, believed, and received his father's love.

There is an unspoken question left dangling in the air by the father to his oldest son: *will you dare to be loved as I long to love you, or will you insist on being loved as you feel you ought to be loved?*[7]

What makes the father's backyard conversation with his legalistic, judgmental son so incredible is how unfair it is.

What makes the father's sprint down the sidewalk to his wayward, narcissistic son so amazing is how unfair it is.

Grace is unfair.

If you are like me, you tend to hold up a strainer and say,

"I can only receive so much grace at a time."

When we say this we, in effect, judge God by telling Him how much love we should or should not receive. Or how much grace others should or should not receive.

I was walking by a store and saw a big sign that said I should stop in because they were offering something for free.

I kept walking.

"Nothing is free," I told myself.

If it's too good to be true, it's too good to be true.

In a consumerist society, this seems to be a pretty good principle to live by.

I wonder, however, if this becomes part of our problem when it comes to interacting with God.

I wonder if the greatest obstacle to redemption is that we just can't accept a love and a salvation that are free.

It would seem that God has a difficult PR job.

The difficulty is in giving Himself away.

Not because He is mean or unkind ... but because He is simply *too* good.

When we learn to accept grace—unfair, wild, and inequitable as it can seem sometimes—we learn a little something about redemption. God redeems only those who realize that they cannot make it without Him. This breaking news about God's love and rescue is called "the gospel." It seems that the gospel is only good news if we are in need of good news.

A LIFE REDEEMED

My friend Bill told me he likes to go on long drives and think about attending his funeral. He imagines who will be there and who won't.

He sits on the fourth row and listens to people talk about what he meant to them and how he impacted their lives.

He said sometimes he breaks down crying.

No one has ever accused Bill of being normal.

While Bill thinks about the end of his life and falls apart in tears of joy and sorrow, many think about the end of their lives and feel fear. This fear can come from many places, but one place this fear is emphasized is in certain religious circles.

I'm not sure how often you think about the end of your life (or if you have the vivid imagination that Bill does), but it can certainly be healthy to look back and recognize redemption.

This is the great hope of humanity.

This is the secret of those who live with joy.

God does not delete your story—*He redeems* it!

We are on a continuous quest for something more. God allows others into your story, even those who hurt you, to reveal something about truth.

This journey begins with awareness and culminates in joy.

When we look back through the lens of how we have moved, how we have become unstuck, how we have learned to love well, something becomes clearer than ever before.

We have received something we didn't deserve and something we all long for in the center of our being.

Redemption.

AN UNEARNED GRACE

Once upon a time there was a baby prince.

His grandfather and father are killed in the same battle.

A new king takes the throne.

In light of the change in political climate, the baby's nurse fears for the little one's life and runs off with him. Unfortunately, in her haste, she loses her balance, and he falls from her arms. The baby lands awkwardly and severely injures both feet.

He screams. She scoops him up and runs.

Eventually, the nurse finds a cabin in the wilderness, where she raises the child, keeping him hidden from the new regime.

The baby prince is disabled. He grows up, his life characterized by fear and shame.

He has lost not only his honor but also his dignity. A prince who cannot walk, run, or ride.

He feels he is of no value. Not only will he never live out the dreams of his royal family, he cannot even contribute to society. He has no sense of identity or worth. There are no fairy tales waiting for him. He is like a soulless container taking up space, waiting his turn to die.

One day a man who knew his father comes to the door. This stranger says that the new king has personally asked to see him.

Terrified but obedient, the young man makes the trek to the palace.

He is met with an extraordinary surprise. The new king welcomes him and immediately puts him at ease. The king speaks with authority but also with a great kindness, and he says something so impossible to believe that the shunned and handicapped former prince kneels before the king, wide-eyed and bewildered.

The king tells him that he wants to give him great wealth.

And not only that, but the king wants him to join the royal family at the dinner table for meals, as if he was the king's own son.

The disfigured boy blurts out, "Why me?!

"I have nothing to offer. I live in a barren wasteland—which is an adequate metaphor and reality of my life.

"I do not deserve this."

The king stands, calls him by name, and draws close.

"Mephibosheth, you have heard the stories, haven't you?

"Your father was my best friend.

"I realize much time has gone by, and I have been busy at war, but I made a promise to your father that I would take care of his family.

"I am adopting you. You are an outsider no more.

"I know this is a grace you did not deserve or expect—that is what makes it grace. It is given freely. Given to you, because you are your father's son."

And so ...

the impaired outcast became a prince once again

and spent the rest of his life

dining with the king.

That is a true story.[8]

THE TENSION OF GRACE

It is painfully difficult for us to accept something that we did not earn.

Grace is what separates the teachings of Jesus from every other world religion. Other religious systems ascribe to a form of accounting, whereby our behavior or works guarantee the approval of the gods and establish a place for us in the after-life. We must do something to deserve salvation.

Not so with the God of the Bible.

With grace, we do nothing. We don't deserve it, and we cannot gain it, win it, build it, or buy it for ourselves.

Grace sits on the precipice of an eternal choice.

Accept it, and live in the wild, uncontrollable love of God.

Reject it, and choose to live without that love. Choose to live isolated in your dysfunction in a state of perpetuity. I wonder if that's what hell is? You getting to have eternity isolated and alone with yourself, with all of your dysfunction and evil tendencies left unchecked, a never-ending cancerous tumor squeezing out any memory of goodness ...

Hell is just a freely chosen identity based on
something else besides God going on forever.[9]

Tim Keller

Have you ever said, "I can never forgive myself"?

Think about what that statement means.

It means that more must be done. You must atone.

Somehow you must pay.

And so you administer self-punishment:

I will not smile.

I will not experience joy.

I will not be happy.

I will not experience love.

The problem is, you can never do enough. You cannot deny yourself enough. You and your behavior are simply not enough payment.

Anyone who spends life in pursuit of this kind of atonement will tell you so. There is no peace. Only malevolence, loneliness, and despair.

The only one who could make that payment for you would be someone who was perfect. Someone who could offer Himself as a substitute.

Jesus was that someone. He gave His life for you, me, Angie, Bill, and Mephibosheth.

Was it enough? That is the real question.

Here is the challenge with accepting God's grace. We have no control over our destiny, though some would argue that we all live under an illusion of control anyway. If we accept the grace that God so freely offers, then we surrender. We stop fighting.

> *Often those who reject the message have greater*
> *fears that there might be a haunting truth to*
> *it than those who claim to believe it.*[10]
>
> Ravi Zacharias

Religious people especially have trouble with this.

They prefer tribalism and control.

If grace is at play, then their powers of manipulation are vanquished.

Grace is scandalous.

It is terrifying for control freaks.

But not for loving fathers.

A FATHER'S GIFT

As a dad I like to give gifts.

I do a lot of mission work with orphanages around the world. While traveling I try to find small gifts to bring back to my family so they know they were on my mind.

On a trip to China, I found amazing headphones that I could never afford in the States. They were inexpensive in this foreign country, so I bought some for Angie, my three oldest children, and me. My family was blown away. They said the headphones were their favorite gift of all time! One day at school, Jordan put his backpack down and jumped into a pickup game on the soccer field. When he retrieved his bag, he noticed that his beloved headphones were gone. Jordan was crushed. He came home in despair. I couldn't afford to replace them. There was nothing I could do.

Later that night Jordan asked me, "If I save up enough money, can I buy your headphones from you?" It was a responsible question.

He didn't presume that he deserved another gift.

What he didn't know was that I had been having conversations with God about the loss. I sensed God prompting me to give Jordan my headphones.

I argued with God about it. The conversation went something like this:

"Seems like You're suggesting I give up my headphones. Not sure that is a good idea. Don't You think this is a great opportunity for Jordan to feel the weight of disappointment?

"Not everything goes according to plan in this world.

"Bad things happen.

"When something is stolen from you, the feeling of violation is awful, but it could be a whole lot worse, right?

"I am thinking this could be an important life lesson for Jordan.

"I am thinking he should probably live in the tension and feel the weight of loss.

"He will think more responsibly before leaving his backpack to play ball.

"He will be more aware in the future, he will ..."

(Pause)

"God, it doesn't sound like we're tracking. You want me to do what?

"Are You sure that's a good idea?"

God's response: *Yes.*

Me: "Aww, man."

I liked my headphones.

While thinking about how to give them to Jordan, I was also working on a message about grace. I spoke in front of our church that Sunday.

In the middle of the talk, I asked Jordan to join me on the stage.

I told the church how Jordan lost his headphones and how disappointing it was. Jordan just stood there sheepishly. I talked about how he had asked to buy mine. Then I looked at my son.

I told him that I felt compelled to give him a gift.

I turned, opened a box, and pulled out my headphones, which happened to be the exact same color as his.

"Jordan, this is my gift to you."

Jordan had thanked me for his headphones the first time around. He knew he'd done nothing to deserve them, but he also knew his father to be a loving father who gives his children gifts.

And then Jordan had something stolen from him.

The undeserved gift.

When I gave Jordan the same headphones the second time around, he broke down and cried in my arms. While we stood onstage with our arms around each other, he whispered in my ear,

"Thank you, Dad, thank you."[11]

As a father, a thank-you is more than enough.

AMAZING GRACE

While on the drive home from church, Jordan could have
been tempted to say,

"Is there something I can do to earn this?

"This is too much for me to receive."

I would say, "No, nothing."

Grace.

The law says, "Jordan, you will first clean out the garage,
then the yard, then the house. After this you will make sure
that every item in your room and closet is in its perfect place,
arranged in perfect geometrical patterns, according to like
colors. And you will do this daily without fail. If you do this
with precision, without faltering, you can earn this gift." The
foregone conclusion is that he would never fully fulfill his obli-
gations. This expectation, this "law," would never be perfectly
executed. It would forever expose Jordan's inability to live up
to my expectation. God gave us the law first to prove to us
that we cannot do it on our own.

This is the same concept Jesus taught and John the apostle
reiterated: if we have hatred in our heart for another, we have

committed murder.[12] Our heart reveals our insufficiency. Our imperfection. We cannot be good enough on our own.

There will always be a temptation to create a formula and trivialize grace.

The loving Father and God of the universe did more than just give up something that was beneficial, something He delighted in—like I did with a pair of headphones. He gave up His Son.

For you and for me. He gave us life. Salvation.

We don't get to downplay it by earning it. It's too big.

We don't get to make it small enough to explain with our finite minds.

It is infinite.

"The salvation story is a God story.... He does not consult us regarding matters of timing.

This requires constant iteration. We humans, with our deep-seated pretensions to being gods, are endlessly preoccupied with worrying and tinkering with matters of salvation as if we were in charge of it. But we are not. God carries out the work of salvation; not, to be sure, without our participation, but it is God's work done in God's way."[13]

A church father, St. Augustine, who appeared on the scene about four hundred years after Jesus, said that pride is the mother of all sins.

Every moment you stay longer in your shame, every moment you refuse to receive forgiveness, every moment you refuse to accept grace is a moment of pride. It's the cartoonist's rendering of us shaking our fist at God, saying, "There must be something I can do to earn this!

"Something in me must be good enough!

"Something in me must be equivalent to You!"

The eternal treasure of the universe, one each of us must unearth in his or her own way, is the astonishing discovery of unfathomable freedom found in the deep mystery of God's relentless grace.

REDEMPTION STORY

God has an ability to take every moment of your life and turn it into gold. The horror, the abuse, the neglect, the abandonment, the shame, the lust, the greed, every awful thing done to you and every awful sin committed by you—turned, reshaped, reformed, purified, and reframed in redemption. When you surrender, His story becomes your story, and yours His.

> *He gives beauty for ashes*
> *Strength for fear*
> *Gladness for mourning*
> *Peace for despair*[14]
> Crystal Lewis

Have you ever wondered about the church's fascination with sculptures and images of Jesus on a cross? A crucifix is the symbol of Jesus completing the work of redemption.

> *But he was pierced for our transgressions,*
> *he was crushed for our iniquities;*
> *the punishment that brought us peace was upon him,*
> *and by his wounds we are healed.*[15]
> Isaiah the prophet

The figure of the God-man, limp on a cross.

Not because life was over.

But because the redemptive work was completed. Jesus said, "It is finished."[16]

The world and its inhabitants can be fully rescued and restored to their original design.

God is not just passively tolerating and observing human suffering—He is participating in it.

"Jesus is, in effect, saying, *This is how evil is transformed into good! I am going to take the worst thing and turn it into the best thing, so you will never be victimized, destroyed or help-less again! I am giving YOU the victory over death!*"[17]

Throughout our struggle, there were moments when Angie and I felt unworthy and unloved. The feelings often vacil-lated back and forth between us, but at different times, with our broken lives in our laps, we felt as though we couldn't go on.

We wondered how God could really love such broken people and how in the world He would ever fix our mess.

We learned that we had to continually die to our own agenda and timetable for how we thought everything should work. We are learning to accept that we are apprentices, not mas-ters in the Jesus way. We are learning to trust that His ways are often not our ways.[18]

Angie and I went on a journey to find our hearts and live from our souls. It was at times very painful. But that suffering has turned into joy. Not always. Not every day. We still get stuck from time to time and have to find our prompts. But on this side of that journey we love each other more deeply than either of us imagined possible. We receive love and give it away. More often than we realize, in our deep gratitude to our loving Father, a smile sneaks across and a tear leaks out, and our faces give away a new attitude of the soul. We are awake and are deeply passionate about carrying His love story to the world.

What about your story?

What gives your life value?

Where do you find hope?

Are you in need of rescue?

Do you know what it is like to be loved well?

You are amazing and unique.

The day you were born, you were an endangered species.

One of a kind.

Absolutely no one on the planet has your story.

Refuse to let the voices in your head and the volume of the world drown out your significance.

Yours is a life worth living. Yours is a story worth telling. Cast aside the shame, lift up your head, and stride with dignity.

You are an adventurer. Your existence proves our need for you. You fit into this divine mosaic. You and me. Our broken-ness alongside the brokenness of others creates beauty. Be a receiver of grace. Be a recognizer of redemption.

From the seeds of surrender sown into the now-fertile soil of your life, God will bring sustenance. *Certainly God was and is a constant gardener.*[19]

This is not the end. Fully embrace the life you have been given. Go now, and love well.

1. Stuck? Say it. Acknowledge it. Open your eyes.

2. Stuck? Do something new. Find resistance and push through it.

3. Stuck? Eliminate distractions. Create space and feel.

4. Stuck? Identify the obstacle. Speak out shame.

5. Stuck? Set boundaries. Learn to say no.

6. Stuck? Recognize the value of suffering. Feel through your pain.

7. *Stuck? Listen to someone else's story. Be vulnerable with yours.*

8. *Stuck? Take inventory. List what you have learned.*

9. *Stuck? Forgive. Stay open to connection.*

10. *Stuck? Receive love. Give yourself away.*

11. *Stuck? Enjoy life. Celebrate the little things.*

12. *Stuck? Reflect. Receive grace and be confident in redemption.*

EPILOGUE

I believe we have been designed to be generous with our lives.

We are to be Purveyors of Truth.

Heralds of Story.

Whisperers of the Way.

Givers of Life.

Lovers of Love.

Carriers of the Spirit of God to the world.

I have two-thousand-year-old breaking news:

The dramatic story we find ourselves in? I know the Author.

And He is good. He is good. No, really—He is good.

Predictable in His character, unpredictable in His expression.

He is writing a masterpiece. He has included you and me.

I get to be a part of the writing process.

Sometimes I screw up the story line. I mean, badly.

Totally go off on a theme He never intended.

And then, when I submit to Him, He writes it in. I mean, the whole thing.

And somehow, it enhances the story He was writing from the beginning. What was unintentional is suddenly intentional. How can He do that?

What if I told you that in the chaos of the world and its geo-political maneuvering, its economics, its historic unraveling ... what if I told you there was a stream of absolute truth?

A rhythm that, when discovered, is not dissonant,

but melodic and harmonious.

And that it is found in a relationship with Truth.

Not just a knowledge of truth, but a relationship with Truth.

Jesus Christ. God Incarnate.

If you are willing to exit the Matrix,

if your soul will slow down or stay awake long enough,

you will be able to see the Story at play around you.

The purpose of your existence, the originality, the unique design that makes you. You will find focus, at least for a season, and you will receive glimpses of what you were created to be and what you will one day become.

You may stay in your denial, believing ignorance is bliss, or, possibly in your shallow desire for current pleasure, you may choose to ignore the dissatisfaction in your soul.

But that doesn't mean it's not there.

And remember this: if you do give your life back to the Designer who designed you, if you place yourself in the hands of God, your desire for wholeness will never be fully quenched this side of heaven. The book of Hebrews speaks of flawed people who stepped into the story and believed.

The writer said:

> These people were still living by faith when they
> died. They did not receive the things promised;
> they only saw them and welcomed them from a
> distance, admitting that they were foreigners and
> strangers on earth.[1]

If you choose the way of faith, forgiveness, and love, you will experience peace, joy, and the overwhelming grace of God. Life never remains the same. It will continue to pass from one season to another. At any given moment you may be thrown backward, wondering how to navigate life's freshest struggle.

Equipped with a new set of tools and a life awakened to Love, trust the one who has saved you. Live in a continual surrender and constant recalibration to the ways of Jesus.

Do you hear that? It sounds like a knock on the door. It sounds like someone is waiting for you. Go—there is a Captain with a meal prepared and a ship waiting. Live your adventure as only you can.

And maybe one day, in a far-off distant land, we will all sit around a campfire together.

You, me, Angie, Doyle, Joseph, Aunt Sally, and a woman with an empty alabaster box.

Oh, and I imagine there might be one more in our midst. The Great Storyteller.

We will listen intently as He has a new story to tell.

NOTES

INTRODUCTION

1. Mark Nepo, *The Exquisite Risk* (New York: Three Rivers, 2005), 12.

CHAPTER 1: NUMB

1. Brené Brown, "Brené Brown: The Power of Vulnerability," TED, June 2010,
http://www.ted.com/talks/brene_brown_on_vulnerability.html.
2. Anthony de Mello, *Awareness* (New York: Doubleday, 1990), 5–6.
3. Brent Curtis and John Eldredge, *The Sacred Romance* (Nashville: Thomas Nelson, 1997), 4.
4. All Sons & Daughters, "Reason To Sing," *Season One* © 2012 Integrity Music. Used with permission.
5. Mark Nepo, *The Exquisite Risk* (New York: Three Rivers, 2005), xiii.
6. John 10:10.

7. Steven Pressfield, *The War of Art* (New York: Black Irish Entertainment LLC, 2002), 15.

8. Proverbs 4:23 KJV.

CHAPTER 2: A RELUCTANT NAVIGATOR

1. Thomas Aquinas, *Summa Theologiae* (Cambridge, UK: Cambridge University Press, 2006), 200.

2. Wallace Stegner, *Where the Bluebird Sings to the Lemonade Springs* (New York: Random House, 1995), 181.

3. J. D. Greear, *Stop Asking Jesus into Your Heart* (Nashville: B&H, 2013), 5.

4. Matthew 25:40.

5. James 1:27.

6. Richard Rohr, *Breathing Under Water* (Cincinnati: St. Anthony Messenger, 2011), 9.

7. Philippians 1:6.

8. Hebrews 11:1 KJV.

9. Young, *The Cost of Certainty* (Cambridge, MA: Crowley Publications, 2005), 6.

10. John Ortberg, *The Me I Want to Be* (Grand Rapids: Zondervan, 2010), 23.

11. Erwin Raphael McManus, *Seizing Your Divine Moment* (Nashville: Thomas Nelson, 2002), 67.

12. Proverbs 6:6 NASB.

CHAPTER 3: PUT ASIDE THE RANGER

1. Mike Mason, *Practicing the Presence of People* (Colorado Springs: Waterbrook, 1999), 1.

2. Thomas Merton, *Contemplation in a World of Action* (New York: Doubleday, 1971), 346.

3. *The Lord of the Rings: Return of the King*, directed by Peter Jackson (Los Angeles: New Line Cinema, 2003).

4. William James, "Is Life Worth Living?" *The Will to Believe and Other Essays in Popular Philosophy* (New York: Dover, 1956), 59.

5. Hans Urs von Balthasar, *Prayer* (San Francisco: Ignatius, 1986), 16.

6. Shlomo Riskin, *Torah Lights* (Jerusalem: Maggid Books, 2009), 188.

7. Sue Monk Kidd, *When the Heart Waits* (New York: HarperCollins, 1990), 22

8. Kidd, *When the Heart Waits*, 37.

9. Wendell Berry, *A Timbered Choir* (Washington, DC: Counterpoint: 1998), 14.

10. Genesis 2:1–2.

11. Lawrence Kushner, *Jewish Spirituality: A Brief Introduction for Christians* (Woodstock, VT: Jewish Lights, 2001), 84.

12 Eugene Peterson, *Christ Plays in Ten Thousand Places* (Grand Rapids: Eerdmans, 2005), 117.

13. Richard Rohr, *Everything Belongs* (New York: The Crossroad Publishing Company, 2003), 62.

14. Mark Nepo, *The Exquisite Risk* (New York: Three Rivers, 2005), 59.

CHAPTER 4: THE NAMELESS WOMAN

1. Robert McKee, "The Story Seminar," lecture, Loyola Marymount University, March 2010.

2. Abraham Joshua Heschel, *I Asked for Wonder*, ed. Samuel Dresner (New York: Crossroad Publishing Company, 1983), 67.

3. Malcolm Forbes, *The Sayings of Chairman Malcolm* (New York: HarperCollins, 1978).

4. Eugene Peterson, *Christ Plays in Ten Thousand Places* (Grand Rapids: Eerdmans, 2005), 144–46.

5. Brené Brown, *I Thought It Was Just Me* (New York: Penguin, 2007), 23.

6. Luke 7:39.

7. Luke 7:40–42, author's paraphrase.

8. Luke 7:42.

9. Luke 7:43.

10. Luke 7:44–47.

11. Ronald Rolheiser, *The Holy Longing* (New York: Doubleday, 1999), 133.

12. Luke 7:48, author's paraphrase.

13. John Fischer, *12 Steps for the Recovering Pharisee* (Grand Rapids: Bethany House, 2000), 49.

14. Brown, *I Thought It Was Just Me*, 13.

15. Dan Allender, "Marriage and Family," lecture, February 2, 2011.

16. Richard Rohr, *Everything Belongs* (New York: Crossroad Publishing, 2003), 21.

CHAPTER 5: STONE FENCES

1. Simon Sinek, *Start with Why* (New York: Penguin, 2009), 17, 28.

2. Charles Swindoll, *The Grace Awakening* (Nashville: Thomas Nelson, 2010), 39–40.

3. *Codependency*: the fallacy of trying to control interior feelings by controlling people, things, and the events on the outside, as well as constantly looking for feedback from others. To the codependent, control or the lack of it is central to every aspect of life.

4. Dan Allender and Tremper Longman III, *Breaking the Idols of Your Heart* (Downers Grove, IL: InterVarsity, 2007) 17, 33.

5. Galatians 5:1.

6. Henry Cloud and John Townsend, *Boundaries: When to Say Yes, How to Say No to Take Control of Your Life* (Grand Rapids: Zondervan, 1992), 32, 35.

7. Cloud and Townsend, *Boundaries*, 31.

8. Robert G. Barnes, *Ready for Responsibility* (Grand Rapids: Zondervan, 1997), 66–70.

9. Cloud and Townsend, *Boundaries*, 36.

10. Cloud and Townsend, *Boundaries*, 26–27.

CHAPTER 6: THE GIFT OF SUFFERING

1. Mark Nepo, *The Exquisite Risk* (New York: Three Rivers, 2005), 34.

2. *Monty Python and the Holy Grail*, directed by Terry Gilliam and Terry Jones (EMI Films, 1975).

3. Tim Keller, "Forgiving Grace," sermon, Redeemer Presbyterian Church, New York City, January 20, 2002.

4. Marcel Proust, *Remembrance of Things Past*, trans. C. K. Scott and Stephen Hudson, vol. 2 (Hertfordshire, UK: Wordsworth Editions Limited, 2006), 131.

5. Source unknown.

6. John 12:24.

7. Nepo, *The Exquisite Risk*, 47.

8. Richard Rohr, *Everything Belongs* (New York: Crossroad Publishing, 2003), 120.

9. Henri Nouwen, *The Inner Voice of Love* (New York: Random House, 1998), 103.

10. Richard Rohr, *Things Hidden* (Cincinnati: St. Anthony Messenger, 2008), 44.

CHAPTER 7: TELL ME A STORY

1. Muriel Rukeyser, *The Speed of Darkness* (New York: Random House, 1968), 111.

2. Robert Putnam, *Bowling Alone* (New York: Simon and Schuster, 2000), 331.

3. Eugene Peterson, *Christ Plays in Ten Thousand Places* (Grand Rapids: Eerdmans, 2005), 30.

4. Mark Nepo, *The Exquisite Risk* (New York: Three Rivers, 2005), 5.

5. Larry Crabb, *Soultalk: Speaking with Power into the Lives of Others* (Nashville: Thomas Nelson, 2003), 160.

6. Curt Thompson, *Anatomy of the Soul* (Carol Stream, IL: Tyndale, 2010), xiv.

7. James 5:16 NLT.

8. Brian McLaren, *Finding Our Way Again* (Thomas Nelson: Nashville, 2008), 147.

9. Psalm 32:3–5 MSG.

10. Robert McKee, "The Story Seminar," lecture, Loyola Marymount University, March 2010.

11. Ecclesiastes 3:11.

12. Hebrews 10:24.

13. Brené Brown, "The Power of Vulnerability," TED, June 2010, http://www.ted.com/talks/brene_brown_on_vulnerability.html.

CHAPTER 8: LIFE IS A SETUP

1. William James, *The Principles of Psychology*, vol. 2 (London: Macmillan, 1891), 369.

2. Genesis 37:20.

3. Genesis 37:21–22, author's paraphrase.

4. Genesis 37:26–27, author's paraphrase.

5. Tim Hansel, *You Gotta Keep Dancin'* (Colorado Springs, CO: David C Cook, 1985), 55.

6. Genesis 39:7, author's paraphrase.

7. See Genesis 39 for the full account.

8. Jeff O'Leary, *The Centurion Principles* (Nashville: Thomas Nelson, 2004), 99.

9. Genesis 40:8, author's paraphrase.

10. Genesis 40:19, author's paraphrase.

11. Genesis 40:13–15, author's paraphrase.

12. Genesis 40:23, author's paraphrase. See Genesis 40 for the full account.

13. Genesis 41:25–27, author's paraphrase.

14. Genesis 41:33–36, author's paraphrase.

15. Genesis 41:38–39, author's paraphrase. See Genesis 41 for the full account.

16. James 1:2–4.

17. Psalm 119:105 KJV.

CHAPTER 9: REUNION

1. Paula Huston, *Forgiveness* (Brewster, MA: Paraclete Press, 2008), 13.

2. Genesis 41:47–52.

3. Genesis 42:1–2.

4. Enmeshment between a parent and child will often result in over-involvement in each other's lives so that it makes it hard for the child to become developmentally independent and responsible for his or her choices.

5. From the film *Life of Pi*.

6. Genesis 42:10–11.

7. Genesis 42:19–20.

8. Genesis 42:21.

9. Genesis 42:24.

10. See Genesis 42:24–25.

11. See Genesis 42:27–36.

12. See Genesis 42:37–38.

13. See Genesis 43:8–14.

14. Genesis 43:15–18.

15. Genesis 43:27.

16. Genesis 43:28.

17. Genesis 43:30.

18. See Genesis 43:31–34.

19. See Genesis 44:1–2.

20. See Genesis 44:3–10.

21. Genesis 44:14–16.

22. See Genesis 44:18–32.

23. Genesis 44:33–34.

24. Genesis 45:1–2.

25. Genesis 45:3a, author's paraphrase.

26. Genesis 45:3–4.

27. Genesis 45:4–5.

28. Genesis 45:14–15.

29. Philip Yancey, *What's So Amazing about Grace?* (Grand Rapids: Zondervan, 1997), 93.

30. Tim Keller, "Forgiving Grace," sermon, Redeemer Presbyterian Church, New York City, January 20, 2002.

CHAPTER 10: LOVE LONGS TO BE KNOWN

1. Dan Allender and Tremper Longman III, *Bold Love* (Colorado Springs: NavPress, 1992), 32.

2. A. W. Tozer, *The Pursuit of God* (Radford, VA: Wilder Publications, 2008), 26.

3. Eugene Peterson, *Christ Plays in Ten Thousand Places* (Grand Rapids: Eerdmans, 2005), 327.

4. Rob Bell, *Sex God* (New York: HarperCollins, 2012), 89.

5. 1 John 4:18.

6. Anthony de Mello, *Awareness* (New York: Doubleday, 1990), 54.

7. 1 John 4:16.

8. Ed Wheat and Gaye Wheat, *Intended for Pleasure* (Grand Rapids: Revell, 1977), 22.

9. Luke 15:11–20.

10. Henri Nouwen, *The Return of the Prodigal Son* (New York: Doubleday, 1992), 36.

11. Luke 15:16.

12. Luke 15:20.

13. Luke 15:21.

14. Luke 15:22–24.

15. C. S. Lewis, *The Lion, the Witch and the Wardrobe* (New York: Collier, 1950), 76.

CHAPTER 11: JOY-FULL

1. Ronald Rolheiser, *The Holy Longing* (New York: Doubleday, 1999), 221.

2. Galatians 5:22.

3. John Ortberg, *The Life You've Always Wanted* (Grand Rapids: Zondervan, 1997, 2002), 64.

4. Leslie Jordan, David Leonard, and Jamie George, "So Safe, So Sound."

5. Psalm 118:24 ESV.

6. Dictionary.com, s.v. "joy," http://dictionary.reference.com/browse/joy?s=t.

7. Rolheiser, *The Holy Longing*, 27.

8. Philippians 4:4 ESV.

9. Anthony de Mello, *The Way to Love* (New York: Doubleday, 1995), 89.

10. Lamentations 3:22–23 KJV.

11. Erwin McManus, *The Barbarian Way* (Nashville: Thomas Nelson, 2005), 15–17.

12. Matthew 12:34 WNT.

13. C. S. Lewis, *Reflections on the Psalms* (New York: Harcourt, 1958), 90, 93–94.

14. Bill Murray, interview by Geoffrey Macnab, "I Know How to Be Sour," *The Guardian*, December 31, 2003, http://www.theguardian.com/film/2004/jan/01/1.

CHAPTER 12: FRAMING REDEMPTION

1. Hans Urs von Balthasar, *Prayer*, trans. by Graham Harrison (San Francisco: Ignatius Press, 1986), 18.

2. Philip Yancey, *What's So Amazing about Grace?* (Grand Rapids: Zondervan, 1997), 61.

3. Herbert Kretzmer, "Stars," *Les Misérables* (musical).

4. See Matthew 7:3.

5. Luke 15:29.

6. Luke 15:31–32.

7. Paraphrased from Henri Nouwen, *The Return of the Prodigal Son* (New York: Doubleday, 1994), 97.

8. See 2 Samuel 9. Some elements of this story are adapted from Charles Swindoll, *The Grace Awakening* (Nashville: Thomas Nelson, 2010), 56–64.

9. Tim Keller, "Hell" (sermon).

10. Ravi Zacharias, *Jesus Among Other Gods* (Nashville: Thomas Nelson, 2000), 184.

11. To see the videocast of this, watch "Headphones of Grace" at vimeo.com/32162729.

12. 1 John 3:15.

13. Eugene Peterson, *Christ Plays in Ten Thousand Places* (Grand Rapids: Eerdmans, 2005), 151.

14. Crystal Lewis, "Beauty for Ashes," *Beauty for Ashes* © 2002 Metro One/Myrrh Records.

15. Isaiah 53:5.

16. John 19:30.

17. Richard Rohr, *Things Hidden* (Cincinnati: St. Anthony Messenger, 2008), 186, 188.

18. See Isaiah 55:8.

19. Richard R. George, *Marital Death – Marital Life* (Maitland, FL: Xulon Press, 2012), 115.

EPILOGUE

1. Hebrews 11:13.

www.jamiegeorge.com